*Real World*
# TEAMBUILDING
# STRATEGIES

*That*

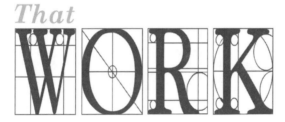

INSIGHT PUBLISHING COMPANY
SEVIERVILLE, TN

Real World
TEAMBUILDING
STRATEGIES
That
WORK

Published by:
Insight Publishing Company
PO Box 4189
Sevierville, TN 37864

Printed in the United States of America

10 9  8 7 6 5 4 3 2

ISBN 1-932863-11-7

# Table Of Contents

CHAPTER 1: **Richard Tyler**
Tyler's Ten Essentials for Teambuilding Excellence™.............. 1

CHAPTER 2: **Cindy Krosky, LCSW**
Teambuilding Generates Strength ........................................... 31

CHAPTER 3: **Margie Thomas, CTC**
Why Is Teamwork So Hard?...................................................... 55

CHAPTER 4: **Terry Wall, CMC**
Teambuilding Is Everyone's Business ..................................... 79

CHAPTER 5: **Jan Baller**
A Step Beyond: Building High-Performing Teams ................ 101

CHAPTER 6: **Dr. Jacalyn Sherriton & James L. Stern**
Beyond Blindfolds: Teambuilding That Works ...................... 133

CHAPTER 7: **Kristi Valenzuela**
It's A Jungle Out There! Team Survival Strategies
For Today's Tribes ................................................................. 159

CHAPTER 8: **Lee S. Johnsen**
Balancing The Scales Of Team Leadership........................... 177

CHAPTER 9: **Karen Phelps**
The Wheel Of Teambuilding Fortune ..................................... 207

# A Message From The Publisher

Some of my most rewarding experiences in business—or in my personal life, for that matter—have been at meetings, conventions or gatherings, after the formal events have concluded. Inevitably, small groups of ten to fifteen men and women gather together to rehash the happenings of the day and to exchange war stories, recently heard jokes or the latest gossip from their industry. It is in these informal gatherings where some of the best lessons can be learned.

Usually, in informal groups of professionals, there are those who clearly have lived through more battles and learned more lessons than others. These are the men and women who are really getting the job done, and everyone around the room knows it. When they comment on the topic of the moment, they don't just spout the latest hot theory or trend, and they don't ramble on and on without a relevant point. These battle-scarred warriors have lessons to share that everyone senses are just a little more real, more relevant and therefore, worthy of more attention.

These are the kind of people we have recruited for the *Power Learning* series of books. Each title offers contributions from men and women who are making a significant impact on their culture, in their field, and on their colleagues and clients. This edition offers a variety of themes in the area of teambuilding strategies. It is ripe with "the good stuff," as an old friend of mine used to always say. Inside these pages you'll find ideas, insights, strategies and philosophies that are working with real people, in real companies and under real circumstances.

It is our hope that you keep this book with you until you've dog-eared every chapter and made so many notes in the margins that you have trouble seeing the original words on the pages. There is treasure here. Enjoy digging!

# Chapter One

## Tyler's Ten Essentials for Teambuilding Excellence™

### Richard Tyler

The challenges and opportunities that face us today are more complex than they have ever been. The mind-bending pace of emerging technologies, the runaway speed of communications and our own insatiable demand for more precision, higher quality and more options, leaves us in a new place. We operate today in a world that demands collaboration and multiple levels of expertise. One reality that has not changed is that individuals feel valued when their unique talents, expertise and experiences are combined with those of others to achieve a common goal. I have found that organizations that operate outside this reality are quickly becoming extinct.

There is no question that many organizations today not only recognize the value of effective teamwork but they embrace it as a guiding principal. There *is* some question, however, about how well we really understand the concept.

After all, we have all overused the phrase "team player" for so long that it has essentially lost all meaning; if you ask ten people to define it, you'll get ten different answers. Yet for all the stated commitment to collaboration and team development, there is a surprising lack of fundamental education on the topic. As youth, we may have participated in team sports and learned many valuable lessons about working with others to achieve a common goal; but those experiences only scratch the surface of the kind of education that is necessary to be an effective team member on the job. And the skills necessary to be an effective team member are different from the skills necessary to be an effective team leader.

This chapter is designed as a framework for teambuilding fundamentals. It is written for the team leader, but the lessons are applicable to every team member. It is divided into ten segments, which we will call **Tyler's Ten Essentials for Teambuilding Excellence™**. These lessons are immediately actionable to help you jump-start your performance.

Whatever occupies your attention, it is likely that some form of effective collaboration with others will significantly improve your chances of a successful outcome. If you will slip this reference guide into your Tyler's Excellence Toolkit™ and *commit* to building Teamwork Excellence, you will be well on your way to guaranteeing your success.

**First things first . . .**

Before we jump into Tyler's Ten Essentials™, a key question—one of the *first* questions—that team members will wonder, if not express aloud is, "Why are we here?" And although this question too often goes unanswered, it is exactly the right first question. In fact, I believe the most important first exercise a team can perform is to ask the right starter questions:

1. **WHY are we here?** That is, why is this group being assembled? If you're not sure, you're not ready to assemble the team. Leadership is about being confident, sure of the

desired outcome, respectful and genuinely interested in the people brought together to make it happen. Don't pull your team together until you can answer this question quickly and confidently.

2. **WHO are the members of this team?** Sounds simple, right? It's the people around the table, the ones called to this meeting. Well, not so fast. How many times have you been in a situation where you've either thought, whispered or blurted out loud something like, "Where's Barbara? Shouldn't the head of IT be on the team that will be evaluating the latest IT strategy?" Maybe. Maybe not. It depends ultimately on the particular purpose of the team, which is exactly why this question should always be asked. (We will address this in more detail in Tyler's Essential™ number 5.)

3. **WHAT is the reason these particular members were put on this team?** Again, this question may be obvious, but the excellent team will always ask it. (More on this when we discuss Essential number 4.)

4. **WHERE is the team supposed to be meeting and working?** Whether your team covers several departments or several continents, this is a question to have answered up front. For example, will conference calls, Web meetings or video conferencing be utilized, or will all meetings be face to face?

5. **WHEN will the team be meeting?** How often a team gets together *is not* just an administrative question. Consider this carefully and take your doctor's advice: "Take the minimum effective dose." Meeting for the sake of meeting is a sure way to sap a team's energy and enthusiasm. Respect the group's time and make the most of it.

6. **HOW will the team perform its job?** Defining responsibilities and making clear how the team will go about achieving success is crucial. If everyone clearly understands the standards by which the team will operate as well as the

associated expectations, the team's effectiveness will go up exponentially.

Keep these six points in mind as we step through **Tyler's Ten Essentials for Teambuilding Excellence™**.

## Tyler's Team Essential™ #1—Set Excellent Team Goals

I have often heard it said that teams fail because they fail to set goals. I disagree. My experience has taught me that teams, successful or not, almost always set goals. In fact, most teams instinctively set goals at their first meeting. Unfortunately, these goals are often purely administrative or inconsequential goals that distract the team from setting appropriate goals. I have found that the reasons for this range from lack of team leadership to the team members' need to reduce uncertainty. "Okay, then, we've agreed that our first goal will be to achieve a ninety-percent or better participation level at each of our team meetings..." Without the right guidance, teams get so focused on setting and enforcing inconsequential goals that they can lose sight of the reason they've been brought together—or worse, *never understand why they have been brought together*.

> **Teams don't fail because they fail to set goals; they fail because they don't set the *right* goals.**

I believe that teams fail, not because they fail to set goals, but because they fail to set the *right* goals.

In order for a team to be a success, it must set goals. After all, isn't that the real definition of success—the achievement of goals? Each member of the team needs to clearly understand the team goals as well as how they relate to the company's corporate goals.

Goals focus on results, not actions. You may have heard that all goals should be "**S.M.A.R.T.**"—Specific, Measurable, Attainable, Relevant to mission and Timely. Let's review how each of these attributes relates to building an effective team.

## Specific

This small word is the difference between a good goal and a vision. "I would like to see world peace," is an admirable vision, but it is not specific enough to be a goal. A good goal will point the team members in a precise direction. Everyone who hears the goal, whether on the team or not, should be able to understand the meaning of the goal well enough to determine whether or not it has been achieved. "By the end of this decade, we will put a man on the Moon and return him safely to Earth." John F. Kennedy's famous speech set a specific goal, the achievement of which was easily able to be determined.

## Measurable

How can you know you have gotten there if you don't know where *there* is? Some goals are easy to measure, like the increase of sales by a certain percentage. Other goals may require you to gather feedback from the team or from your customers. For example, if your team's goal is to increase customer satisfaction, you may need to develop a customer feedback survey in order to determine how satisfied your customers are now and how much that level of satisfaction changes as a result of the efforts of the team. Regardless of the effort required, do not launch a team into action without first determining how you will measure success.

## Attainable

Nothing will frustrate a team more and keep them from succeeding than an unrealistic goal. "We will increase sales by fifty percent in thirty days," sounds big, but it may not be motivating at all if it is impossible. This is where team goal setting will really help. The members of the team will be able to determine if an individual's goals are too lofty and not in the realm of possibility. However, my experience has taught me that teams will often be even more aggressive than the leader initially planned. By asking the team to set the milestones, you not only get quick buy-in, you often get bigger achievement!

## Relevant to mission

The goals should relate to the purpose of the team. Why was it formed? What is the overall mission of the team, and how does this relate to the mission, purpose and corporate goals of your company or organization? If there are inconsistencies, your team members will be confused, and their loyalty may be divided.

A friend of mine told me he once served a key role on a change-management team for a very large corporation. The team was made up of the highest profile, highest flying employees in the company and led by the company's president. Sounds like a recipe for sure success, right? Not in this case. The initiative was the president's pet project, but unfortunately, he was on his way out. The team members were conflicted, because there was clear disparity between the company's new mission and the outgoing president's vision. The team was, by all accounts, a miserable failure, and the otherwise worthwhile initiative never got off the ground.

## Timely

The only way that a goal can be measured is to know "when" as well as "what" you are working to achieve. All action steps that are created as a result of planning to meet the team's goals are built around the estimated completion date of the work. A goal to improve customer service is only valuable if you articulate how you will measure improvement and the time frame within which the improvement must occur.

How do you set team goals? To reiterate, *you* don't! The team does. While it is certainly true that you should have a clear idea of the ultimate goal in mind before ever pulling the team together, the interim steps, the milestones, the additional strategies should all come from the full team. Oftentimes, the reason for the team's existence is to solve a problem. Determining *how* that problem is resolved is a team activity. Brainstorm with the team to arrive at the "how." Remember that in brainstorming, you should ask the question that is the most relevant to the team's purpose. For example, "What would we need to do to maximize our sales growth this quarter?" The question you use will determine how comprehensive your goals are and if they will support the goals of your company or organization.

Encourage participation in this goal-setting session by reminding the team that everyone's ideas are important. Get everyone's ideas out, have the team select the top five or ten goals, and then fine tune them using the S.M.A.R.T. technique. Ask the team to review the goals and determine if anything is missing. Continue this until every member of the team is satisfied that the goals are well defined and comprehensive.

Finally, with team goal setting, the most important part is to have good follow through. I have found that a responsibility chart and periodic review of the results help to keep a team on track. A responsibility chart helps you determine who is primarily responsible for a goal or a portion of a goal and who is there to assist that person. A responsibility chart also ensures a more equitable distribution of work and builds agreements that involve the whole team (see Table 1.1). I recommend letting the team complete this chart. Although it may be more time consuming than doing it yourself, getting the team involved will help achieve a stronger commitment and a more solid understanding of how the goals will be achieved.

**ESSENTIAL CHECKLIST:**

1. Establish the most important result(s) your team must achieve.

2. Bring the team together to help define "the state of the union"—that is, where you are today relative to the result(s) you want to achieve.

3. Bring the team together for a separate meeting to brainstorm the ways (the interim steps you can take) to get from where you are today to the desired result(s).

4. Apply the S.M.A.R.T. technique to transform these interim steps into achievable goals.

5. Assign specific responsibility for these goals on a responsibility chart to be shared with all members.

Table 1.1 Sample Responsibility Chart

| Goal | Completion Date | Team Member 1 | Team Member 2 | Team Member 3 | Team Member 4 | Team Member 5 |
|---|---|---|---|---|---|---|
|  |  |  |  |  |  |  |
|  |  |  |  |  |  |  |
|  |  |  |  |  |  |  |
|  |  |  |  |  |  |  |

## Tyler's Team Essential™ #2—Identifying Team Priorities

The first step in setting team priorities is for every member of the team to have a clear understanding of the team goals. Use active listening to make sure all the team members are committed to these goals. Next, look for personal agendas.

Tom, a team leader with a national company, asked me what to do about the problem he was having with his cross-functional team. The team had been given the responsibility of looking at the company's employee benefits and suggesting improvements, with the goal of becoming a more attractive work environment and thus making recruitment of top talent easier. The team member from accounting wanted to make the cost of the benefits the number one priority, while the team member from information systems wanted the priority to be a system that was easy to administer. Both were important perspectives, but how could Tom get his team to forego personal agendas and remain true to the task that was assigned? Of course, the benefits package needed to be cost effective and efficient, but the team was charged with determining what benefits prospective employees would find most important.

I suggested he consider "stretching" his team members by having the accounting person look at the systems analysis and the information systems team member review costs, while the rest of the team researched the question of value-added benefits.

---

**"Never doubt that a small group of committed people can change the world. Indeed, it's the only thing that ever has."**

*Margaret Mead*

---

**Eliminating personal agendas** on your team is *necessary* before your team can set its priorities. After doing this, use the same brainstorming process to prioritize the goals set by your team. Next, take each goal and evaluate the challenges that the team may face as it seeks to accomplish that goal. Anticipating these challenges will result in action steps to eliminate obstacles. Those action steps will be a team priority. In other words, before the team can accomplish a goal, all obstacles to that goal will need to be eliminated.

The next step will be to make **action plans** for each goal. Breaking large goals down into small, manageable actions will motivate the team and eliminate the inactivity that can come from being overwhelmed. It will also be helpful to use a **responsibility chart** to assign team members to individual action steps in the same way you assigned responsibility for goals (see Table 1.1).

**ESSENTIAL CHECKLIST:**

1. Meet with each team member one on one to discuss the team goals.

2. Make note of each person's concerns.

3. Ensure that each team member clearly understands the goals and is ready to support the team's level of commitment.

4. Use this meeting to make the final decision as to whether each member is appropriate for the team (an uncommitted team member that has too tight a grip on a personal agenda can quickly spoil the team's ability to be effective).

## Tyler's Team Essential™ #3—How to Tie Personal and Professional Goals to Team Performance

Once you have established team goals and priorities, you will turn your attention to the individuals brought together to achieve these goals. Clearly, each member is different and yet, as the leader, you need to get each person equally motivated to provide excellent performance. You may have imagined (or even given) a magical, Vince Lombardi-like motivational speech intended to instantly inspire each person to peak performance. If you've ever used this approach, think about how it actually went. My guess is that it didn't go as you had hoped; certainly not for the long term.

Why aren't these speeches effective in the workplace when they seem to work so well for great coaches? The problem is that, unlike the football team at halftime, your team will likely be playing longer than two hours. Your team's goals will likely be more complex, and the team members will be juggling other responsibilities and have other loyalties. An adrenalin-stirring speech to your team may motivate them for the short term, but by itself, it is not an effective long-term solution to keeping the team members effectively on task.

One way to capture your team members' attention and keep them motivated is through **personal development planning**.

By helping your team members formulate **personal development plans**, you will be helping them establish personal and professional goals that improve their own performance and accelerate the achievement of team goals. You might be wondering if this is really a necessary step. If your team is to be together for longer than a couple of months, I believe the answer is an unequivocal "yes." Make no mistake: Personal development planning is not easy. It takes time, and initially, it may seem like an unnecessary distraction. But the payoff is big, and it is an essential element of building team excellence.

A **personal development goal** is one that *improves the individual's life*. An example of this would be the goal of becoming a more effective communicator, since communication is important in every aspect of life. A **professional development goal** is one that *enhances the performance of the individual's work* or current profession. A member of the real estate department may need to have a professional goal of increasing his or her understanding of stock options, since the team goal this year is to provide stock option benefits to all employees.

Each member of the team will look at each of the team goals and work with the team leader to make an assessment of where he or she needs to improve in order to accomplish that goal successfully. For example, let's say your sales team believes that it would be very valuable to present your product to at least four civic groups per quarter. Sarah is an excellent salesperson and a valued member of the team. Her specialty is one-on-one sales, but she has never been comfortable speaking in front of a large group of people. Sarah decides to set a professional goal of improving her public speaking prior to her turn to speak before a civic group.

The exciting thing about developing the individuals on your team in this way is the win-win nature of the process. An empowered, developed team member is more satisfied and therefore, more productive. Use the goals of the team to develop the individual members, and then leverage the strengths of the members to achieve the goals of the team. When both the team and the individual goals are identified, understood and coupled with a clear action plan, every goal can be achieved.

Table 3.1 and Table 3.2 are samples of goal-setting charts that you can use to help your team develop the personal and professional goals needed to make the team a success.

Table 3.1 – Professional Goal-Setting Chart

| Professional goal: | Relates to which team's goals(s): | Date to be completed by: | Results to be expected: | Measurement of outcome: |
|---|---|---|---|---|
| | | | | |
| | | | | |
| | | | | |

Table 3.2 – Personal Goal-Setting Chart

| Personal goal: | Relates to which team's goals(s): | Date to be completed by: | Results to be expected: | Measurement of outcome: |
|---|---|---|---|---|
| | | | | |
| | | | | |
| | | | | |

## ESSENTIAL CHECKLIST:

1. Have each member identify at least two personal and two professional development goals whose accomplishment will help the team achieve its goals.

2. Have each team member specify his or her goals using the S.M.A.R.T. format.

3. Have the team meet to share goals and action plans. This will build team spirit and will encourage everyone to help each other meet their goals.

4. Establish a regular time for team members to provide updates on personal and professional goal achievements.

## Tyler's Team Essential™ #4—Understanding the Roles that each Team Member Plays

The most basic roles on a team are the team leader and the team members. Each team member can have several roles, depending on the process that the team is undertaking. There are administrative roles, and there are also work- or goal-related roles. The work- or goal-related roles are determined when the responsibility chart is created in the goal-setting process. So let's consider the three key administrative roles that are needed for the team.

### Administrative roles

The team **leader** is typically the first role to be determined. This person will organize the team and ensure cohesiveness and agreement. Creating and maintaining an atmosphere of cooperation and productivity is the primary responsibility of the team leader. The leader communicates the direction or vision of the team, which leads to the formation of the team's goals. The team leader should be mature and confident and should be able to delegate effectively. The most effective team leader is able to identify team members' weaknesses and leverage their strengths.

Another team member should function as the **administrator** of the team. This person will keep all the records and files for the team. The administrator helps the team leader produce meeting agendas, minutes and progress reports and serves as a resource for all information needed by team members.

The third administrative role is the **facilitator**. The facilitator of the team is responsible for all communication, both inside and outside of the team. This person makes sure team members are well informed of what is happening (everyone knows when and where to meet, has minutes, knows the agenda, etc.) and helps the leader manage the team meetings. The facilitator assists in making sure ideas, thoughts and input are recognized and incorporated into each meeting. The facilitator ensures that the meeting stays focused. It is the facilitator's responsibility to clarify ideas for better understanding by all team members. The facilitator also makes sure no one is falling behind and is always on the lookout for potential misunderstandings that require clarification.

## Work-related roles and responsibilities

The work or goal-related responsibilities of the team members are defined in their team job descriptions (if the team has these) and in the responsibility chart for each of the team goals. As the team decides on the work- or goal-related roles for each team member, keep in mind the importance of sharing responsibilities. Encourage the team members to work together to achieve the team's goals. Having the team members share roles for a goal or action step can produce interdependence, a vital part of team synergy.

All team members have certain responsibilities; one of these responsibilities is to discover new areas of growth for the team and to look for alternative methods to work more effectively as a team. Each team member is also responsible for identifying obstacles to the achievement of the team goals, determining the root causes of those obstacles and suggesting solutions to the team. I mentioned that the team leader is responsible for the atmosphere of the team, *but so is every member on the team*. If the team is going to function at peak performance, concerns need to be addressed in a constructive and positive way.

## ESSENTIAL CHECKLIST:

1. Identify the administrative roles and the team members who will fill those roles.
2. Meet individually with the team members whom you've selected to fill these roles to ensure they understand their responsibilities.
3. Meet with the entire team to explain these administrative roles and responsibilities.

4. As the goals are established, assign other team members to work- and goal-related roles.

## Tyler's Team Essential™ #5—Identifying Individual Players and Team Players

The most important decision you can make when building a team is to determine if the people you are selecting will make good team players. Some people—we'll call them "individual players"—function most effectively outside of a team structure. If an individual player needs to be on the team, there are some effective ways to maximize his or her contribution to the team effort.

The first step is to understand the differences between *team players* and *individual players*. To say it another way, learn to identify the attributes of a good team player. I look for **seven key attributes of a team player**:

### "Tyler's Team Player 7"™

1. **A good team player communicates openly** and is not reluctant to present ideas and opinions. He or she keeps the team informed on the work progress and provides positive and constructive feedback to the other team members.

2. **A good team player listens actively**, paraphrasing what is said and seeking clarification from the other team members.

3. **A good team player develops healthy relationships**. Look for people who can initiate relationships with others, who are good at assessing what motivates other people and who value cooperation. Team players who understand the importance of healthy relationships resolve conflict quickly and are very responsive to the needs of others.

4. **A good team player demonstrates patience.** Building a powerful, effective team takes time. The more patient each team member is, the quicker the team will begin to perform

at levels that far exceed the independent efforts of the individuals.

5. **A good team player solves problems.** This is accomplished by generating new ideas, researching trends and evaluating alternatives. The best team players practice these skills unconsciously.

6. **A good team player is very flexible.** In order to solve a problem, a team player needs to recognize that there *is* a problem and that the work or goals of the team may need to be adjusted in order to find a solution. The best team players are people who are open to change and quickly adapt when change is necessary.

7. **A good team player is dependable.** The one characteristic that is admired as much or more than any other is dependability. A person who develops a reputation for doing what he said he would do, being where he said he would be, accomplishing what he said he would accomplish, etc. is the one that every one wants on their team. Think about your most successful teams. Who were the superstars (other than you, of course)? I'll bet the women and men you are thinking of were also the most dependable, right? Think about one of your least successful teams. Did a lack of dependability play a key role in the team's failure?

So, what do you do when you find yourself with an individual player on your team? Some people work best alone. They may consider themselves rugged individualists and see this as a positive characteristic. Indeed, it can be—just not always in a team environment. If your team has individual players on it, and they need to be part of the team, use the personal and professional development process to develop team-player characteristics. Also, consider putting the team player in a role that allows him or her to be an individualist, to go against the grain. Many teams assign a particular player to be the naysayer. You may say to your individual player, "Sue, I want you to play the devil's advocate here. Give us all the reasons why you think this idea won't work." Listen to the individual player, let her know you value her input, and encourage her healthy participation. Often, there are certain aspects of team goals that are best suited for an individual player. Determine your individual player's unique strengths, and then look for places those strengths will benefit rather than hinder the team's progress.

Be sure to communicate with the individual players, and then communicate some more and then some more! The individualists will not seek out information the way your team players will, so be sure they are informed about everything the team is doing, and even consider bringing them into the initial planning process, which can foster faster ownership of the team goals.

Finally, be patient with the individual player on your team. When properly employed, the individualist can well turn out to be one of your top performers.

Visit us at **www.RichardTylerInternational.com**; we have excellent, easy-to-use online assessment tools that can assist you in identifying individual players and team players. Also, look at the ***DiSC® Education*** products at www.DiscEducation.com.

## ESSENTIAL CHECKLIST:

1. Carefully review "Tyler's Team Player 7"™
2. Rate each member of your team using the following format:

Team Member's Name: _____

Characteristic 1: "Communicates openly."

| 1 | 2 | 3 | 4 | 5 | 6 | 7 |
|---|---|---|---|---|---|---|
| Strongly Disagree | Disagree | Somewhat Disagree | Unsure | Somewhat Agree | Agree | Strongly Agree |

Repeat this process for each of the characteristics, and add the total points for each team member. Rank each team member based on total points. Although this will only be one component of your evaluation process, it will help quantify where to anticipate challenges.

3. Meet with the individuals that are most likely to feel uncomfortable in the team environment (the individual players). Share your expectations and concerns, and listen to theirs.

4. Determine how you can leverage the individual players' strengths and mitigate their weaknesses.

5. Schedule time to regularly meet with the individual players to provide and receive feedback. It is very, *very* tempting to focus your attention only on those who rank the highest on your team player list; however doing so to the exclusion of the individual players will exacerbate the independence situation.

6. Use assessment tools to assist you in understanding behavioral characteristics.

## Tyler's Team Essential™ #6—Individual Skills vs. Team Skills

If you have watched a highly successful team at work, you may have noticed that it's not always easy to find the superstars. It's also often hard to make a distinction between individual and team performance because the two are so well integrated. This may be easiest to see in sports. The teams that make it to the top and stay there are often the ones that have no obvious superstars but rather a team full of them. The key to the sustained success of the team is that they have learned to turn individual skills into team skills.

Every person on a team comes to the team with individual skills. The team itself has no skills until the individuals begin contributing in a productive way. I mentioned that the most common mistake teams make, which is often fatal to the team's success, is failing to set the *right* goals. **The second most common teambuilding mistake** is the failure to recognize that individual skills must be transformed into team skills. Sounds good, but how do you actually do it?

One of the most important first steps is to use teambuilding activities to reveal each individual's expertise to the rest of the group. Doing this early on in the team's formation will create mutual respect for what each person brings to the team and will set the stage for cross-training the team members.

---

**The second most common teambuilding mistake:** *Failure to recognize that individual skills must be transformed into team skills.*

---

As the team performs its work, have individuals share their unique knowledge and skills with the rest of the team. This will enrich the team and create the wonderful synergy that makes teambuilding worthwhile. There are several ways to encourage team members to share their individual expertise with each other.

One way is to pair up team members to perform tasks that require the use of skills held by one member of the pair. Make it clear to both team members that this is an opportunity for the knowledgeable partner to share with the other person and that you expect both people to perform the work.

Another way of encouraging the sharing of knowledge and skills is to have a team member report on his or her progress to the whole team. Again, communicate to this person that you would like him to educate as well as inform. Remind the person to avoid technical jargon and to translate the information into general language for the group.

If members are reluctant to share their knowledge, it may be because they believe they have nothing unique to offer the team. Your responsibility is to identify why each member of the team was selected and make clear why those skills are valuable to the team. It is also a good practice to identify the high flyer—the team member that seems to be performing at a higher level than the rest. Point out this excellent performance to the team without putting down anyone's performance and challenge others to rise to new standards of performance.

The more knowledgeable the team members are about their own skills and the skills of others on the team, the more successful the team will be at achieving its goals.

## ESSENTIAL CHECKLIST:

1. Make sure each team member understands why he or she has been selected to serve on this team.
2. Make sure the whole team understands the skills that each individual brings to the team.
3. Structure activities so that individual expertise is taught to other team members. This will improve the expert's skill level as well as improve the team's overall skill level and performance.
4. Find the one or two members of your team who are outperforming the others, point them out to the team, and challenge everyone to meet the performance.

## Tyler's Team Essential™ #7—Team Operations–The Communications Link

A team that takes communication for granted, or flat-out ignores it, will never achieve excellence. The most important step you can take when forming your team is to establish a communication plan and then get the team members to commit to it. This isn't to say that you must have the perfect plan in order to be effective; in fact, you should all agree that the plan will regularly be revisited to evaluate ways it can be improved.

A communication plan will make clear to the team the process by which challenges will be solved, decisions will be made and communication will occur. In other words, a good communication plan smoothes and significantly improves team operations. Working with your team to answer the following questions will help you create the right communication plan for your needs:

1. When will team meetings be held?
2. How will their effectiveness be evaluated?
3. What are the team guidelines for making decisions?
4. How will information be communicated to the team? (E-mail, weekly update meeting, telephone, etc.)
5. How will team and individual feedback be given? (Will there be a process or venue for regular feedback?)
6. What current team policies work well?
7. Which policies (if any) hamper individual performance?
8. Which (if any) are hampering team performance?
9. What changes must be made to the policies?
10. Based on the team's experience, what would improve team meetings?

## ESSENTIAL CHECKLIST:

1. Schedule a meeting with one agenda item: Establish (or review) your team's communication plan.
2. With all team members present, define how the team will communicate. Use the questions above as a guide to this discussion.
3. Agree to meet on a regular basis to review the team's communication plan.

## Tyler's Team Essential™ #8—Ensuring Team Feedback

If you ever decide you want to study conflict and human behavior, form a team. Bring people together into any structure and you will see a wide range of interests, emotions, motivators, agendas and goals—a perfect recipe for conflict! If you are bringing a group of people together to achieve team goals and you *don't* want to study conflict, then you'll need to focus on setting up a system that ensures team feedback.

Team feedback is really a subset of a good communication plan, but because it is so important and typically so poorly managed, it deserves special attention here. In most team environments, if there is any formal feedback at all, it typically comes to individuals from a single, top-down source—their team leader. When feedback does come to individuals, it usually addresses negative performance. And while there is absolutely nothing wrong with feedback addressing negative performance, the excellent team will have a formalized system for providing peer feedback from all team members regarding team performance as well as each individual's performance—*both positive and negative.*

The best time to establish an effective feedback structure is during the formation stage. Because the individuals are looking for how the team will work together and are interested in the rules by which the team will operate, a feedback structure will be more readily adopted. However, even if your team has been together for years, the process can be effectively integrated into the team communication structure.

The process for establishing a solid feedback structure is not complicated, but it does take careful planning. Whether you are forming a new team or are leading a team that's been together for a long time, you can plan teambuilding activities designed to encourage open communication. You can also use the goal-setting and goal-achieving process to craft a performance feedback structure. In other words, use the work of the team to build the team.

---

**If you ever decide you want to study conflict and human behavior, form a team.**

---

If the responsibility chart and the action steps are clearly assigned, feedback can be equally clear and objective. If it is my responsibility to deliver a completed assignment to the team on the fifteenth of this month, and all the members of the team *know* this is my responsibility, measuring my performance is an *objective* exercise. However, if the delivery date is "as soon as I can get it completed," then measuring my performance becomes a *subjective* exercise and thus a potential source of conflict. So build that foundation when developing the team goals by assigning responsibility.

In addition to using clearly measurable goals to provide feedback, you should also establish a peer-review methodology. This includes requiring individual team members to provide feedback on their own performance, the team's performance and the other team members' performance. Start by having the team compile a list of attributes of an excellent team player. You can use **"Tyler's Team Player 7"**™ to start discussion and build from there. Have the team members rate their own performance (see Table 10.1 as a guide for this team discussion), and then rate each of the other members. If the team is new and the members have no experience with the others on the team, this will be a more effective exercise later. But you should establish the expectation up front that this process will be an ongoing component of ensuring team excellence.

You should review these feedback forms to look for any obvious discrepancies between the individual's self assessment and the peer assessment of his or her team readiness. This will help you with **personal development planning**. Encourage team members to share feedback with each other, and then ask individuals to share their feedback with the group: In what areas do the peers see them excelling? What are the ways the peers believe their performance can be improved? Ultimately, the goal of a feedback structure is to ensure open, frank communication among members. Your job is to establish an environment in which feedback is encouraged, constructive and accepted. Each team is different. I have seen teams adopt this kind of process immediately and run with it. Other teams have required significant coaching. Regardless of how much time it takes to integrate this process, stick to it. An excellent way to coach is to *model the behavior* you would like to see. Have your team provide you with feedback on your performance and accept it *without being defensive*. You will be creating a safe environment for providing feedback, and you will improve your performance as the team leader.

When your feedback system is well integrated into the team structure and a part of team expectations, it is like gold. I guarantee it will strengthen your team and improve performance.

## ESSENTIAL CHECKLIST:

1. Schedule a meeting with your team for the sole purpose of establishing a feedback system. Get input from the team as to the components they would like to see become parts of the system. Openly discuss their concerns about such a system.

2. Get your team to provide you with feedback about your performance and use that to create a safe environment for open feedback.

3. Require team members to assess their own performance as team players.

4. Establish a peer-review system that requires team members to rate one another's performance.

5. Review feedback forms to identify any potential discrepancies requiring attention.

6. Integrate the feedback process into team meetings.

## Tyler's Team Essential™ #9—Team Dynamics–The Importance of Values

Each team member must work well with other members to achieve excellent results. If the team is merely a collection of individual players, then the performance will never reach its potential. By creating a well-defined communication plan that incorporates a solid feedback structure, you will have a great vehicle for converting individual performance into team performance. However, there is still one critical component that must still be addressed—the importance of values.

Each of us has a set of values that guides us in all that we do. For some, those values are loosely defined; for others, they are very clearly defined. In either case, when individuals are asked to participate on a team, they don't check their values at the door and adopt "whatever the team thinks." During a team's first few meetings, its value system will begin to emerge. This value system will determine how team members interact with one another, how aggressive or conservative the team will be, how responsive, how focused on improvement, how open and so on. And all of this happens whether the leader is involved or not. *Please don't miss the importance of this*: If you want to build an excellent team, you need to understand the importance of values, and you need to be involved in helping the team define its value system.

I have found that one of the best ways to do this is to have the team set standards as early as possible. By asking the team members' opinions on various value positions, you will see individual preferences emerge, and you will be able to move toward "value matching." Value matching is the process of matching individual team members' values with one another to establish standards that the team agrees to adopt.

Develop your own set of safe and potentially controversial topics for exploring individual value positioning. A safe topic question might be, "On a scale from one to seven, how important is it that each team member participates in team activities?" A potentially controversial topic might be, "On a scale from one to seven, how important is it that Team Member A let the team leader know when Team Member B is not pulling his or her share of the load?" Come up with some of these kinds of questions and have some fun with it.

The point here is to let the team know why you are doing it and get them involved. You might kick off such a meeting by saying something like,

> *"We all need to decide together what this team's core values will look like. We'll consider these our guiding principles of success. To do this, we'll need to decide what is important to us individually and how that will impact our method of achieving our team goals. It is critical that I have everyone participate in this process.*

*I'll start with some questions, but I need everyone to get involved, come up with their own questions and get them on the table."*

You will find this exercise very enlightening, and it will go a long way to bringing the team closer together. The result of this process should be a written set of core principles or values that guides the team's efforts to reach performance excellence and achieve its goals. One area that should be clearly defined is that unethical, immoral or illegal behavior has no place in the team's value system and will not be accepted from any team member. Any behavior such as this will taint or destroy any good work product that comes from the team.

## ESSENTIAL CHECKLIST:

1. Schedule a "value-matching" meeting—if possible, early in the life of your team.
2. Let the team know why you are meeting and lead off by asking a few value-position questions.
3. Ask each team member to come up with his or her own questions.
4. Reach agreement within the team on the standards that will guide their efforts.
5. Put these standards in writing, present them to the team members and review them frequently.

## Tyler's Team Essential™ #10—Evaluating Who Makes an Excellent Team Member

The following inventory is designed to help you evaluate your capabilities as a team player. The only way this will be a useful tool to you is if you answer the questions as objectively as you can. For those areas where you believe there is room for improvement, outline a plan of action that will help you improve your performance. It's the same process you will use for your team members. The more you embrace your own personal development, the easier it will be for you to help your team.

Table 10.1 – Team Player Skills Assessment Inventory

*In the left column, record your score based on the following scale:*
1 – Strongly Disagree
2 – Disagree
3 – Somewhat Disagree
4 – Uncertain
5 – Somewhat Agree
6 – Agree
7 – Strongly Agree

_____ My communication skills need very little improvement.

_____ I readily accept the goals of others as important.

_____ I am always very flexible.

_____ I readily acknowledge and accept as important the values of others.

_____ I regularly evaluate my own feelings.

_____ I am very open to expressing my feelings.

_____ I am very sensitive to the feelings of others.

_____ I regularly encourage others to express their feelings.

_____ I readily embrace change.

_____ I am very willing to make short-term sacrifices to achieve team objectives.

**ESSENTIAL CHECKLIST:**

1. Objectively assess your team readiness using the Team Player Skills Assessment Inventory.
2. Clearly articulate an action plan designed to improve those areas you believe require improvement.
3. Ask team members for objective feedback and ask specific questions designed to target those areas you believe require improvement.
4. Schedule time to regularly review your personal and team member assessment of your performance and your development plan progress.

The process of forming and leading a team of any size for any duration is a challenge. Achieving **Teambuilding Excellence** is a lifelong pursuit. That pursuit of excellence begins with taking your responsibility as a team leader—or team member—seriously. For those who commit to excellence, the success that can be achieved through team effort is extraordinary.

I leave you with two thoughts. The first: To be a masterful team leader, you *must* understand and master teambuilding dynamics, so enroll in a team-buidling education program and reap the rewards. The second: **"Remember that your success tomorrow is in direct proportion to your Commitment to EXCELLENCE™ today."™**

## About The Author

### Richard Tyler

Richard Tyler is the CEO of **Richard Tyler International, Inc.™** an organization named one of the top training and consulting firms in the world. Mr. Tyler's success in sales, management, leadership, quality improvement and customer service and his reputation for powerful educational methods and motivational techniques, has made him one of the most sought after consultants, lecturers, teachers and success coaches. Mr. Tyler shares his philosophies with millions of individuals each year through keynote speaking, syndicated writing, radio, television, seminars, books, compact discs and tapes. Mr. Tyler's book *SMART BUSINESS STRATEGIES*™, *The* Guide to Small Business Marketing *EXCELLENCE* has been hailed as one of the best books ever written for small-business marketing. His successful books include; *Leadership Defined*, *Real World Customer Service Strategies That Work*, *Real World Human Resource Strategies That Work*, *Real World Teambuilding Strategies That Work*, *Conversations on Success*, *Conversations on Customer Service & Sales*, *Conversations on Health & Wellness*, *Conversations on Faith*, and *Marketing Magic*. His philosophies have been featured in *Entrepreneur Magazine*® as well as in hundreds of articles and interviews. Mr. Tyler is the founder of the **Leadership for Tomorrow™** an organization dedicated to educating young adults in the importance of self-esteem, goal setting and life-long success. He serves on the Advisory Board and is past Board Chairperson to **Be an Angel Fund**, a non-profit organization helping multiple handicapped children and profoundly deaf children to have a better life.

**Richard Tyler International, Inc.™**
P.O. BOX 630249
Houston, TX 77263-0249
phone: (+1) 713-974-7214
email: RichardTyler@RichardTyler.com
website: http://www.RichardTyler.com
website: http://www.TylerTraining.com
website: http://www.ExcellenceEdge.com
website: http://www.DiscEducation.com

# Chapter 2

## Teambuilding Generates Strength

### Cindy Krosky, LCSW

To be successful, companies must be proactive in maximizing the performance of their most vital resources—the people who represent them and work with them. Companies are realizing that in order to remain competitive in the marketplace, they must think outside the fish bowl and entice more people to swim with them instead of against them. The days of relying on "business as usual" are history. In order to be productive, leadership needs to appreciate employees instead of using a management approach that depreciates them. Businesses must shift gears and move outside their comfort zones.

One of the best ways to move a company into the new century and away from old habits is to provide teambuilding initiatives and exercises that physically take staff away from the work scene. Away from the traditional work environment, there is an opportunity to discover the internal resources that are often hidden behind desks, equipment and formal job titles. In this new environment, a team can experience in one day what it may take years to completely implement in the work setting. Because a team approach is often new to people, we have to get them to taste this approach and develop a thirst for it. Without the desire to create a team, there will always be people who resist the change and look for ways to undermine the team.

In the last two decades, management has realized the importance of using a teamwork approach instead of a dictatorship. The old method of leading is gone; it is no longer "My way or the highway." Today, people will leave managers who rule instead of lead. Attempts to motivate people with fear are unproductive as this creates dissension and animosity instead of cohesion and honesty in the work environment. Management that leads realizes that teamwork increases motivation and productivity. Helping people to think as a team and to work as a team requires some understanding of how people learn as well as how they adjust to change.

Much of our life experience has inadvertently taught us to work alone. In school, students battle against each other for scores. When people are not working together, they are in competition with one another. This competitive behavior is often ingrained in us through sports, academic settings, at home or at work. In most of these settings, there really is only room for one person at the top. Many children and adults have had overwhelming exposure to activities that play one person against another. These activities endorse a strategy of opposition, a belief that it is important to defeat other people. This makes competitive thoughts and reactions a first response and teamwork a last response. Thus, increased education about, exposure to and acceptance of the teamwork concept all require development.

"Team" is a four-letter word that many people have misused; sometimes it is perceived as a dirty word. One of the reasons that the team concept is often a challenge to apply in the business world is our lack of practice in using it in other areas of life. The initial exposure to the team concept typically begins at home and at school with the introduction of sports. These brief exposures to open teams fall short of giving most of the working world firsthand experience with a team concept. Outside of professional athletes, less than twenty percent of the entire U.S. population over the age of seven participates in a team sport (U.S. Census Bureau). Is it any wonder why this concept is foreign to many people?

Too often, people use "team" as a label for a group of people sharing a common task. This obviously adds to the misuse of the term and increased misunderstanding about what it means to be a team (as opposed to a group). The word "team," by definition, means people working together to reach a common goal, versus working on a common task. Teams seek cohesiveness and work so that their actions complement each other as they seek to strike a balance that respects the diversity of the members and therefore strengthen the synergy that exists in the team. On the other hand, people working as a group generally take an individual approach to issues. Group members discuss individual views, identify individual concerns and often are stuck looking at the problem instead of seeking the solution.

So how do leaders help people become team oriented? Acknowledgment and awareness are the first keys to tackling the problem. Denying that a problem exists will not improve the situation. Sometimes denial is based on the misunderstanding that people working as a group are actually functioning as a team, and this may not be the case. So carefully examine how problems are approached to help decipher if members are acting as a team or as a group.

Whether you are trying to create a team or reenergize an existing team, a little adventure can go a long way. Reality Oriented Physical Experience Services (ROPES), also known as adventure-based training, promotes the team-approach philosophy. ROPES initiatives are as physically and mentally challenging as any work project a team can encounter. The outdoor environment that best suits adventure programs offers participants a chance to shed office titles and other work barriers. Adventure-based programs build team cohesiveness by promoting strong team skills. ROPES initiatives promote teamwork by actively engaging participants in the learning process since many people learn better when they are physically engaged in the learning process.

## Elements Needed for a Team

Trust is one of the most important elements in teambuilding. It is an element that must be continually nurtured and maintained through each phase of the process. Without trust, we destroy all of the strides we make. In this chapter, I will be introducing concepts and ways to use an adventure-based approach to help introduce or reinforce the concepts so that members build trust and gain a thirst and desire to be a team. People learn by doing. The experiential nature of this training meets the needs of various learning styles and thus permits diverse groups of people to grasp the concepts and learn how to correct problems faster.

Adventure-based teambuilding is an exciting and powerful experience, specially designed to foster self-confidence, self-discovery, trust, open communication and group cohesiveness. Managers who have never been on a team learn to become team players and better coaches. Employees work out personal differences, find strengths on which to build and learn how to improve their ability to trust one another. These are only a few of the accomplishments that can occur in adventure-based training. Activities present both physical and mental challenges by using a three-step approach to move a group of people through the stages of team development.

1. Briefing—introduces the activity, rules and guidelines for the activity

2. Adventure-based activity—the planning and completion of the activity

3. Debriefing—reviews the process of the planning and how it was executed

To improve processes, quality and productivity, it is important that the team be driven by conviction and a technical knowledge of the task at hand. Participants in a successful project must also know how to plan, gather information, communicate results, implement changes and work as a team. Continuing business pressures to achieve and expand require that management look at integrated teamwork as a daily expectation from employees. While many people already possess the skills to be team members, the group as a whole may need some fine tuning on social skills in order for the team to work cohesively. Training on interpersonal skills increases each member's awareness of how to work with diverse populations of employees who work next to one another. While there is diversity culturally, politically and socially, diversity across generations often has an even greater impact on the ability of people to communicate, share, solve problems and get along. A lack of respect or understanding between people with any differences immediately creates a barrier. Thus, the group as a whole may need some fine tuning to be productive.

## People in the Formation of Teams

In order to increase the potential of our most vital resources—the people—businesses have to learn more about their employees and the skills that each person has that can enhance the growth of the company.

With organizational resizing being a trend of the future, the "good ol' boy" belief that "people will remain a part of the team because we hired them" is a thing of the past. Uncertainty reigns more fluently through organizations today. Therefore, it is increasingly vital for businesses to improve communication through all the levels of the organization and to increase each person's understanding of the role he plays within the department, the organization and the team. An efficient team understands synergy and the benefits of cooperation. Personal job satisfaction is increased among employees when they understand their roles and when they are permitted to function cohesively as a team.

Teams take time and energy to create. There is no magic wand that creates a perfectly formed team. Many different elements impact the building of a team, such as leadership during the growth of the team, the corporate culture's view of team importance and the social skills that are possessed or needed by team members. Since the team process is more effective if it is accepted and promoted from the top down, the person(s) leading the team process should possess the skill, patience and understanding of this transformational process.

## The Four Stages of Teambuilding

Building an effective team occurs in stages, because people must accept and adapt to the process of working as a team. It is essential to understand the dynamics of how people interact to move properly through these stages. It is unlike any other process that businesses are accustomed to introducing. There is no manual to give members to read so that they will magically and suddenly work and function as a team. But while we cannot just teach people to be a team, we can teach them what social skills are needed to be effective team members and what it feels like to be a part of a team. The easiest way to offer this education is to let team members experience it. In adventure-based training programs, participants experience the team concept and are able to adjust and enhance their skills as they develop some of the people skills they may need. Each person responds differently to the process, but there is still some predictability to the stages that the people will experience.

The first stage is **Forming**, when the team initially comes together and the people are simply a group of people who have different questions, different agendas and no feeling of connection to other members. The next stage is **Storming**, in which there is an emerging of cohesiveness among some members. A sense of direction is beginning to be accepted by the end of this stage. There is a decline in the "What's In It For Me? (WIIFM)" question. Following this stage, teams will move into the **Norming** stage, where goals are clearer and trust among members has increased. At this stage, there is a level of comfort among members and a desire to work together for the good of the idea or product instead of for self-gratification. The final stage is the **Performing** stage, where there is trust among the team members and they hold one vision or goal that has been accepted by everyone on the team. The team focus is on quality versus credit.

---

**It is amazing how many problems can be resolved when we do not worry about who gets the credit for the solution.**

---

All of these stages take time. People who have never had experience in a team setting rarely believe that it is possible to take the chaos that reigns during formation and tame the competitive nature of people to create a cohesive team of people seeking a common goal.

## Forming a Team

Wouldn't it be great to get your team on course from the start, to shorten the learning curve and gain some valuable tools to increase the team momentum and decrease the team delays? On the adventure-based course, teams have the chance to learn and improve skills that will keep them on track.

When teams first meet, the leader or facilitator should have team members list skills that they need to be a part of a team. Before groups of people form teams, or when existing teams want to succeed, they must know the skills that are required and agree to work on building and maintaining them. Brainstorming the team skills permits each member to identify the elements that are necessary for this particular group of people to function cohesively. Listing the skills increases each member's awareness of using these skills. It is similar to making out a grocery list before shopping to increase the likelihood that what we purchase will include the items we need. Making a list of team skills increases the participant's awareness of what is needed and increases her mental alertness to identify and exhibit the skill—or at least realize that the skill is missing and needs to be developed.

Next, the leader or facilitator should identify goals, both personal and team oriented. Goals are important, because they give direction to the people who set them and to the team as a whole. These skills and goals should be referred to at strategic points in the meeting, during the adventure-based activities

37

and in the briefing and debriefing sessions of the activities. With skills and goals in place, many groups choose to incorporate the use of a Full-Value Contract or Team Agreement to increase their commitment to work together. These tools may be designed by the members, but the instrument should contain four key components:

- Acceptance, accountability and a commitment to work together

- Effective communication skills since members need to be willing to give and receive feedback

- Encouragement to work toward team objectives and set goals to evaluate progress in meeting the objectives

- Group discussion and the development of a spirit of forgiveness

Members should be permitted to practice their team skills as they discuss and seek agreement on the contract. Therefore, it is important that the contract/agreement should be written in terms easily understood by all members of the team. Once the group has reached a consensus, the members should sign the document to represent their united front against the obstacles they will face on the course or in the work setting.

With a contract in place, the team is moving into the Forming stage. There are common goals, knowledge of the skills necessary to meet the challenges that may be encountered and a commitment to stick together. The team should be ready to move forward with a sense of purpose. Leaders should not be fooled by some of the calm that can be exhibited in this first stage, because the games are about to begin.

So where do teams start? A meeting with a trained facilitator should occur before a group comes into the area. This consultation allows the facilitator to understand the goals of the targeted population. An agenda is then created around the specific needs of the organization. Each activity will be structured to incorporate physical, psychological and social challenges. Some of these events will demand that individuals transcend self-imposed limits, whereas others will require sophisticated team cooperation and problem-solving skills. Participants will be instructed to leave their titles, reputations and personal differences at the gate and enter a world where teams are made. Situations will be created to remove people from their normal roles and allow them to take risks with their ideas. The events are naturally fun since people have removed their typical office attire in exchange for shorts or sweat outfits. The magic of the activities creates a bond that will transcend time and location. In this New World, the team will encounter scenarios such as walking above "shark infested waters," balancing over a "cavern" or climbing through "spider webs." Here is where the seeds are planted. People will formulate personal identities on the team, relationships will develop, and an identity as a team will be created.

In adventure-based teambuilding, the Forming stage provides a great environment to let team members learn about one another. On or off the course, it is in this stage of teambuilding that the games will begin. In this initial stage, members test limits, test authority and consistently test the patience of the leader or facilitator. Team leaders and facilitators recognize a group's need to resolve issues that fall into the "interpersonal underworld." They understand that to eliminate undercurrents, a group must spend time on activities that build understanding and support among members. Therefore, meetings or events are often started with initiatives or icebreakers. These interactive exercises allow group members to have fun and get to know each other in a playful way. These activities are generally viewed as non-threatening as there are few, if any, risks. Whether the team is being built in the work setting or outside of work, a group may require more than one icebreaker to break down personal barriers.

In the Forming stage, when teams are first beginning, a communication tool called a sociogram is often used to observe interactive patterns of the members. This tool can be used to objectively document communication dynamics. It provides a more formal record of who participates, who leads conversations and how people interact and respond. Objectively seeing the communication patterns on paper allows team leaders or facilitators to properly use their skills and tools to assure that every member of the team is included in discussions. This tool also provides information about members who may be trying to dominate meetings or who are negative in what they share about the team process. All too often, dominators have a hidden agenda, and if the leader is unskilled in handling these individuals, a leader may travel down the debate path of no return. When this happens, the dominator has thrown the leader off track and thus demonstrated to the other members that the leader lacks the communication skills necessary for a successful team.

---

**Successful teams are not those without problems; rather they are teams that saw the problems, took the challenge and used their energy to find solutions instead of focusing on the problem.**

---

## Communication on Teams in the Forming and Storming Stages

Teams must have basic social skills in order to progress. Communication can make or break a team at any stage. There is good news and bad news about communication. First, the good news is that the ways people speak and listen are learned. Now the bad news: Many people have learned very poor ways of communicating and further develop communication styles that can destroy teamwork. The cadence, volume and tone with which we speak come from our heritage. The vocabulary we use is learned. Expectations are made subconsciously about how people should hear and understand what we say. Rarely do we ask people to paraphrase what we say or ask if clarification is needed. Yet these are all elements of communicating effectively on a team.

---

## Acknowledging our strengths allows us to activate all the potential that already lies within us.

---

In adventure-based training, we start with basics, listening to introductions and then beginning an initiative we call the Name Game. Participants are asked to make some association with their names. These usually reveal some information about how they feel about themselves and how they feel about being a part of the group. This gives the facilitator information on where the team members start and which activities will help them improve their communication skills. It is important that the facilitators establish a basic understanding of each member's communication level. After each activity, the team is debriefed. This is an excellent time to give and receive clarification on communication styles. If the group is talking openly, the next set of activities will test their ability to continue such openness under pressure. Activities used for this stage challenge individuals to remain vocal.

Teams with a great deal of diversity among members need to be aware that communication styles will affect how the team formulates and progresses. Each member has unspoken expectations about how people should hear and understand what is said. Rarely do people practice asking for help or asking others to clarify or paraphrase what was said. Rarely do members take the time to share what helps them listen to a message; generally, people just assume that their communication style works for everyone. As a person who knows cardinal directions—north, south, east, and west—faster than left and right, I am often reminded that unless I ask, what I need to hear in terms of receiving directions is usually not what people provide.

The ability to listen with the intent to understand is another essential element in communication, as is the ability to seek and confirm understanding, or to ask open-ended questions, which will elicit more information. These are all important elements in communicating effectively. Being heard is one thing; knowing you were heard and understood is another.

The facilitator's role is to observe and to step in when needed to bring the team together. This may be done during the activity and at the end of the activity to discuss observations and to facilitate communication among the team members. For example, in an activity called the Tire Traverse, many members approach it as an individual challenge rather than as an opportunity to work together as a team. This activity requires members to traverse from one tire to another over an imaginary ravine. As members attempt to move from tire to tire without touching the ground, it becomes evident that communication is deteriorating as requests for help are stated as demands for help. Members tend to fall back into old habits as anxiety and fatigue challenge their ability to communicate effectively under pressure. Together, the members will struggle through the activity, each knowing what is wanted but also struggling with how to say it or how to ask for it. This is typical behavior for people who are tired or frustrated; they revert to their solo survival skills, choosing not to communicate with or rely on team members. Instead, they expect the others around them to know what they need without having to ask or acknowledging that help is even wanted.

How often have we been guilty of expecting people to know what we need or want of them without asking or saying anything? It seems as if we want people to read our minds so they can fulfill our needs without us having to ask them to help us. Yet we really do not want people around us to be mind readers, because we may have a thought or two that we do not want them to know about. Therefore, the alternative is that we must practice vocalizing what we want or need. We have a responsibility to express ourselves in a manner that shows that we want people to hear our message and that we would appreciate their listening and responding.

Communicating properly is like dancing with a partner. Someone has to take the lead, and the person following has a responsibility to try not to step on his partner's feet. The steps in communication are often confusing; team members withhold help out of respect for the other person's independence and because they, too, struggle to ask if it is okay to give help. In stressful situations, these individuals typically respond with negativity, which tears down communication, instead of admitting the stress is present and just asking for help. This type of poor communication is seen both in and out of the work setting. To prevent this negative cycle from continuing, teams that are Forming or transitioning to Storming teams must be proactive in continually giving and receiving feedback regarding performance.

---

**Developing teamwork is not a one-day experience. It is a daily commitment to seeking excellence, understanding, creativity and cooperation!**

---

The Forming stage of a team can take a lot of time. Moving a team through Forming quickly and efficiently is essential. In the Forming stage, everything takes time and patience. The members are learning what it means to be part of a team and to experiment with their new skills. Adventure activities like the Tire Traverse may take as long to debrief as the activity took to perform. Activities such as this allow members the opportunity to give one another feedback about behaviors and communication styles. Teams in the Forming and Storming stages are still learning the art of giving and receiving feedback. Providing hands-on examples of proper ways to give and receive feedback improves dialogue between team members and helps them improve their ability to offer valuable information.

Feedback starts with pointing out what was done right. The goal of feedback is to be constructive instead of destructive. Feedback builds people up emotionally and professionally, identifying the current skills and ways of using them to improve. By identifying what is being done right, people have a foundation from which they can improve their skills. Constructive feedback starts with what was done right and then identifies ways to make improvements by providing encouragement. Many teams struggle with constructive feedback and attempt to use feedback that is more destructive (this is known as constructive criticism), which only focuses on the mistakes that were made. The phrase "constructive criticism" is misleading, however, because the intent of this message is not to build someone up; it is to tear him or her down. Adventure-based training allows people to practice giving and receiving feedback in a less threatening setting. As suggestions are made, individuals are able to increase their awareness of how they can improve and communicate better with team members. As teams progress through activities, they have the opportunity to improve their communication skills and learn better ways to resolve problems and contribute to the team.

Why should our most vital resource, the people who work with us, trust us enough to want to be on a team with us? What do we know about them, and what have we developed with them to establish at least one ingredient in earning their trust?

Realize that members of a team represent a wide array of generations and cultures, who very likely interpret trust in different ways. Without going in depth into the various reasons why people view trust differently, realize that there are three general ways people give trust:

1. Blind Trust—People trust others because there has never been a reason not to trust that person.
2. Earned Trust—A person's actions and or words have demonstrated that he or she is trustworthy in the eyes of the beholder.
3. Given Trust—These individuals choose specifically when someone will be trusted and to what extent. The trust is given out in increments to determine if the person they are trusting has earned the right to be trusted at certain levels or in certain areas. There is always something being held back, because people do not want to be misled.

Be careful not to judge any of these forms of trust since each of us has used them for one reason or another in our lives.

Realize that trust has several layers, and teams can begin to access and build trust at any level.

## Storming and Communication

The element that facilitates a breakthrough from Forming to Storming is the members' communication with one another. Businesses that participate in the adventure-based program see that the freedom to speak and share is easily created in this artificial environment. Yet the challenge is to allow the lessons learned on the course to be utilized in the work setting. Can these skills be generalized into a business setting? Yes, and they will be, because the groundwork has been laid, and the team has been formed. They have learned how to communicate, how to formulate a plan and how to come to a consensus. The principles applied on the course are principles that apply to life on a daily basis. They are principles that help shape people's lives and enable them to perform to their utmost abilities by improving trust, self-confidence, self-awareness, acceptance and cooperation.

In the Storming stage, feedback is increased and provides a dialogue between team members so that people can identify their positive skills and understand how to improve skills that are weak. For example, in the activity described earlier, the Tire Traverse exercise, we could show in the debriefing that the will to be independent is stronger than the skill to do the activity. One skill to be strengthened is the ability to know when you have reached your limit. The ability to speak out before fatigue and stress take over requires that individuals become willing to do a self-inventory about how they cope with stress. While stress is another subject for another book, it must be introduced here. Stress is the leading cause for deterioration of team cohesiveness or a breakdown in communication at any stage in the team process. Proactive teams provide training in how to decrease stress and thus increase the team momentum.

Team members in the Storming stage increase their listening skills and become intuitive about what their teammates need. Intuition allows people to read between the lines and quickly access what is needed. This does not make a person psychic, but it does allow her to know what others need or want. By appealing to the wants and needs of others, we better align ourselves with our coworkers.

Some people are naturally born intuitors or helpers. They use their intuition about people in the same way most of us use our teeth to chew. People who are not natural intuitors have to work on developing these skills by listening more intensely to understand the deeper meaning of why people are sharing information. Other skills that improve communication are asking open-ended questions that provide more information and repeating what you hear as what you understand, which increases clarity. Once teams move beyond Storming, they can pass entirely through the remaining two stages in less time than it took to get through the initial stages.

### Tying it Together—Moving from the Norming Stage to the Performing Stages

As teams progress, members will demonstrate more cohesiveness as they stop testing limits and let go of the desire to have individual needs met. These early Forming and Storming issues subside as members accept the team in the Norming phase and actively seek unity in the Performing stage. Teams that transition from Norming to Performing are willing to make adjustments and sacrifices for the sake of the team. In adventure-based programs, teams are progressively challenged to demonstrate their mastery in using team skills. Individual members are able to demonstrate how to effectively communicate personal needs while remaining a team.

---

**"Some people succeed because they are destined to, but most succeed because they are determined to."**
**Anonymous**

---

As the team enters the Performing stage and its final development stage, the style of communication and receptiveness to new information becomes more apparent. In the exercises, individuals show how they each communicate personal needs. Further, the team's style of communicating and receiving information can be viewed as a whole.

Glitches occur in both work and in activities. They occur intentionally in activities to ensure that everyone has the chance to lead or at least to be heard. Each situation creates an opportunity for members to be an active part of the plan. When that does not seem to happen naturally, facilitators ensure that it will happen artificially and use it as a key debriefing tool at the end of the activity. Contributions from everyone present are required to reach a goal, even if the goal is getting across a "peanut butter river."

## Storming to Norming

While members are moving from the Storming to Norming stage begin to work more like a team and less like individuals, three I's begin to emerge. The first element is initiative, an invaluable ingredient for team members. Corporate cultures valuing teamwork depend on people taking initiative. Businesses understand the importance of empowering employees to solve problems and to move ahead; thus, they must encourage initiative. Settings, which restrain initiative, decrease the value of teamwork and decrease productivity. Initiative at work can save money, reduce problems and develop a positive work environment, which empowers people to take responsibility.

Team members begin to demonstrate initiative in the Storming stage. In this stage, members are self-starters; they look for solutions when they see a problem instead of just looking at the problem. Do you and your team members possess initiative? Are people encouraged to take initiative when they see a possibility? Teams in the Norming stage readily encourage this skill. People are given permission to solve problems and to take action. They know the boundaries that need to be respected. Demonstrate initiative and others will learn from you! In order for a team to move ahead, the leader must take the first step.

Integrity in what we do and how we do it speaks volumes about who we are as people. Integrity means being honest with ourselves and with others. Sharing what we know is as important as admitting our limitations. Team members and team leaders in the Norming stage have a high level of integrity and trust their teammates. Team members have demonstrated sincerity for those they work with and for. Actions are congruent with the messages people send. People take pride in their work and display their integrity in what they produce.

Initiative, integrity and intuition are essential elements in developing a Performing team. How often do people sell themselves short in life because they are unable to learn one of the three I's? Team members who naturally use the three I's exhibit self-confidence and realize the value of what they offer to the team. Some people who naturally posses them often struggle with providing instruction to teammates who lack one or more of these qualities. It is like a person who excels in math and knows how to get the answer but is unable to simplify the process for the person who doesn't grasp the concept. Every team member needs to take the initiative to develop as many skills as possible to work better with others. We all have areas we can help people with as well as other areas in which we would do better to bring in an outside expert to provide the information. It is never too late for someone to be what they want to become.

**Performing Stage**

When the team reaches the Performing stage, the members have come to realize that each process, each glitch they encounter, even when it is a setback, is still something they can celebrate. The process, and what the team learns in the process, is of equal value to the product or event. Only a Performing team can and will take a moment to realize this and to celebrate what they learned. A team in this stage does not need a pat on the back from people up the corporate ladder. They know they made the mark, and they cheer. Members who make it to Performing stages have better lives on and off the team. At home, they no longer wait to see their child's report card to celebrate an "A"; instead, they celebrate the first "A" on a homework assignment or test. They teach their families to be teams and to celebrate every day. They no longer wait for the team to make the score; instead they cheer when it looks like they are headed in the right direction to score. Then they celebrate again when the score is made.

So why are some people still reluctant to be on a team? It is because the unknown scares most people. Open their eyes and share with them the full benefits of being on a team, and they will never want to go back. But beware! Being on a team is a powerful thing. It will change your work energy, your home life and how you view life. Don't hold back. Go forward, because climbing over obstacles allows us to see the view instead of stare at the wall that blinds us from the view.

### Performing Teams Celebrate: A Real-Life Example

One of my more memorable training programs involved a group of twenty managers from all over the United States, who were working on some teambuilding skills as a prelude to their strategic planning retreat. In presenting them with some adventure-based challenges, we established leadership skills and team skills. These skills included "motivating one another," "celebrating," "giving encouragement" and a host of other skills. This leadership team clearly understood what it meant to celebrate along the way, as they encouraged each person with each step they took and with each step they tried to take. The enthusiasm and ongoing encouragement gave several participants the energy to reach their goals, because they knew people believed in them. When we discussed the accomplishments, the people who cheered and encouraged others talked about how great it was to encourage others and how it personally reenergized them. Perhaps you have cheered a person or provided words of encouragement as she reached for a goal. If you have done this, then you may recall the burst of energy that was ignited within you as you helped celebrate someone else's success. Team members in the Performing stage applaud one another when progress is made.

Don't try to save the energy for the final celebration. Why? Because what if a short-term accomplishment is as close as someone gets to success? Or what if your encouragement could have helped that person reach his potential? Teams know that celebrating and encouraging others along the way lifts everyone up and moves everyone closer to the goal.

I have seen people do what seemed to be impossible feats because people believed in them and lifted them up with open celebration of their successes. It is powerful to watch this occur and be a part of this tremendous success. When we share our encouragement with others, we dare to soar above the ground and live life without regrets, without roots that plant us in old habits, but rather with a level of energy that propels us high above the clouds. Performing teams encourage one another to reach new goals personally and professionally. They tell people today that they believe in them rather than waiting for tomorrow. Celebrate today. Don't wait for tomorrow, because what if today never ends and tomorrow never comes?

## Synergy of a Team

People working as a team use their synergy to get beyond perceived problems and actively seek the solutions. Team members understand it takes everyone working together to discover the solutions and to nurture growth. In business, developing cohesiveness among employees often requires using an expert who can assess the needs of the team and develop a program that will engage the people so that they may develop and adopt a team approach.

Telling people to work together as a team does not make it happen. If words solved the problems, the world would live in harmony, family disputes would cease to exist, and every business that opened would be destined to succeed. However, the reality is that people need education and practice in working functionally as a team.

As a corporate trainer specializing in group dynamics and teambuilding, I find that the most productive training involves interaction—leading people through activities that increase personal and professional awareness of the team concept. Introducing team skills when the group dynamics are in place is vital to moving team members forward to grow and stretch to new levels. The timing of team development progression is essential for everyone. When the group is ready to move forward, each person involved is allowed to relate these concepts to both his personal and professional life. This allows team members to understand how their individual responses and interactions impact other people at work. This experiential approach is very positive and very powerful as the self-realization occurs in a non-intrusive or non-threatening manner, while still allowing the "Ah-ha" to occur. Since each person owns her individual experience, learning is more quickly integrated into her life, and she is more willing to apply what is learned. Practicing what is discovered through interactive activities increases the acceptance and willingness to practice this new behavior in settings and in different areas of her life. As Confucius said: "I hear and I forget, I see and I understand, I experience and I remember."

Part of the debriefing process involves having the participants generalize the similarities of activity scenarios and workplace situations. Making these generalizations is less threatening but still creates the "Ah-ha" moment. In the non-threatening outdoor setting, participants get to identify and address concerns that happened in the activity and then relate them to work so that they can identify ways to prevent similar glitches back at work.

Freedom to speak is created in this artificial environment, but it is up to participants to allow the lessons learned to be used freely in daily work life. Can these skills be generalized into a business setting? Yes, and they should be, because the groundwork has been laid and the team has experienced what it is like to work cohesively. Experiences have provided them with the opportunity to learn how to communicate, how to formulate a plan and how to come to a consensus. They have actively practiced their skills, and now it is time to practice these skills where it counts the most, where the scenarios are real—at work.

These employees have been given the empowerment and the confidence to use their knowledge and skills in the work place. The team has entered a new dimension as they are actually a pro-social community. On the course, the group process was a way of life as people were given support and encouragement as well as recognition for their accomplishments. Because activities on the course are action-centered, it makes tasks associated with the experience action-oriented as well. Explaining to the uninitiated what happens during the day is difficult. However, some explain it by saying that they feel as if there is an aesthetic, archetypal or even spiritually transcendent atmosphere in the environment. You will never know until you try! After all, ROPES can do more than drag you through a process; they can allow you to learn. See you out there!

## About The Author

### Cynthia L. Krosky, LCSW

 Cynthia L. Krosky is a seasoned professional speaker, adventure-based facilitator, licensed clinical social worker, and a certified teacher. Her varied experiences and understanding of group dynamics, enrich her ability to influence the way people work together. She uses her expertise to assist organizations in developing leadership and team skills so that they may discover ways to increase productivity and have fun. Her interactive programs can be provided in a classroom atmosphere, or outdoors in a less traditional environment. Cynthia's programs are regularly presented at national, state, and local conferences and retreats.

Cynthia L. Krosky, LCSW—President
Achieving Corporate Excellence, Inc.
Providing Motivational Keynotes and Training
Office: (772) 461-8313
Web:www.acespeaks.com
Email: acespeaks@acespeaks.com

# Chapter 3

## Why Is Teamwork So Hard?

### Margie Thomas, CTC

Everyone loves a winner. Our society, in particular, loves its champions. Cities compete over professional sports teams; the more successful the team, the harder they try to lay claim to it. A successful team is often a city's crown jewel.

As individuals, we connect with these teams and feel we are part of them. We buy the products of our favorite team's sponsors. We wear the team colors and logos. We are saddened or angered by its losses and elated by its victories. We begin to feel that the team, in some way, owes us a victory. We believe that we can control the team and may even believe that we can do the jobs of the players or coaches better than they can.

I have been an avid Indiana University basketball fan for a long time. During the years that I have watched the team, I have second-guessed the coaches, referees and the players. I have sat in the comfort of my family room, watching the games and wondering (and sometimes verbalizing), "What was going through their minds? Why did the coach substitute that player? Why did he take that shot?" In essence, I have been an armchair coach and player.

## "We like the teamwork idea, but Mr. Superstar won't let us play with his ball."

I will never know what it is like to play college basketball, but for a brief period of time (usually about two hours), I become a part of the team. If you watch or go to any sporting event, you'll see many people who, like me, become a part of their team. You know the ones: They'll paint their faces, wear nothing but official team clothing and give every ounce of their being to support the team. They are true "fan"atics.

I really enjoy watching a team that is playing with passion. You know—the type whose players run down the court celebrating, encouraging their teammates or trying to get the crowd pumped up. It's much more enjoyable than watching a team that simply jogs up and down the court and takes the occasional shot.

Do you have employees who are armchair team members? Do you want them to actively participate in the efforts? Do you want a highly passionate, committed employee or one who just goes through the motions? If you're reading this book, I'm willing to guess that you want passionate and active employees.

So what happened to make your people so dispassionate? As a new manager, I looked at my staff and envisioned a team scoring that last-second shot and winning the championship— in essence, making our business the best. But it never seemed to develop. I gave them lots of rah-rah speeches that would energize them for a short period of time—but never for long. Then I thought I had to "fix" them. So I tried some new quick-fix methods, but these too only lasted for a short time. So I made the assumption that I just had "dead" employees. I began second-guessing what was going on. And because of these assumptions, I focused more on how to cut my losses. I gave the employees only the most basic of tasks. The more creative problem-solving activities I saved for myself. The idea of having them work as a team was frightening. I have spent more than ten years learning that this conclusion and the underlying assumption is wrong:

"Evidently we're not a team! Otherwise we wouldn't have to be at this teambuilding session!"

This statement was made by an individual at a teambuilding retreat. It really caught me off guard and inspired thought. Why did this person think that a teambuilding retreat was a sign that they were not a team? Why do people resist being on teams? Some people are very open and verbal with their feelings about being on a team, while in other cases, they are more passively aggressive about the team effort. In either case, they sabotage the team so they don't have to participate in the team activity.

I believe that as organizations have changed, we have looked to teams as a way of adding energy, commitment and creativity. We have envisioned great victories for businesses only to experience the agony of defeat. And we have needed every individual to willingly participate in these activities. So what are we missing? Why are teams so hard?

## Teams

So what is a team? Webster's New Collegiate Dictionary states that a team is *"a number of persons associated together in work or activity."* Teamwork is defined as *"work done by several associates with each doing a part but all subordinating personal prominence to the efficiency of the whole."*

There has been much written about the different types of teams. In sports, you find football teams, which function differently than basketball teams, which are different from baseball teams. And these teams work totally different than golf or tennis teams.

In organizations, there are also different types of teams. Each needs different support and direction. Are you ready to provide the support? Are you ready to teach the members how to function like a team? I don't mean did you send them to a class to learn to be a team. I mean do you really help them become a team. Do you *coach* your team? Do you possess the skills to coach your team?

It will be difficult, but not impossible, for people who must work independently for most of their duties to become team players for others. In some cases, people will need to completely change or modify their style between the various activities.

For example, sales representatives generally work solo with their clients. They are motivated to sell products; they are paid based on the amount of products they can sell. Fellow employees can be seen as obstacles to these sales and the client seen as more important than the coworkers. Such employee-to-employee relationships can become very confrontational. The various departments (marketing, sales, production, accounting, etc.) take sides in a war instead of working together to help customers get the products or services they need.

This scenario results in situations where finger pointing, blaming and turf protection are commonplace. Usually, the failure of the system ends up on the shoulders of the individual who happens to be at the end of the line. This doesn't make for a creative, energizing environment for the members to solve problems to meet the customers' needs.

Does this have to happen? No. But it will take training, coaching and constant vigilance. Egos need to be checked at the door. The types of questions need to be asked in a less threatening and more informative style. Aimed at gaining information not blaming.

Several years ago, I had the opportunity to watch a manager who was able to make this transformation. Cindy was a very hard-charging individual. She demanded the best of her employees and accepted nothing less. Many employees speculated that her office was stained with the sweat of all the employees who had been raked over the coals when they made mistakes. Employees were paralyzed in fear of making a mistake.

Cindy had the opportunity to attend a training session led by H. Edwards Deming. To say it had an impact on her was an understatement. She went from asking, "Who screwed this up?" (which usually was the last person involved in the process) to "How did this happen?" Being called to Cindy's office or seeing her in one's work area was no longer a scary event.

What was even more exciting was that staff really started looking for areas in which to improve. They weren't frightened of making mistakes. Of course, the innovations had been researched and approved before implementation, and not all ideas were accepted. But the staff was involved, and that made the biggest difference.

What's the environment in your office? Are you looking for the fall guy? Or do you want your employees to be willing to take risks, to research and seek out new ideas and new possibilities? Or do you want them to play it safe and do things the way they've always been done?

If you choose to have more innovative and creative teams, you need to set up a support system and a plan for their success. So let's begin with one of the most crucial pieces.

## The Coach

When I think of a coach, I see someone on the sidelines, intently studying the action, yelling in instructions and encouragement and making adjustments to the team's composition. Some coaches are more animated than others. Some coaches are admired while others are loathed for their style. But they are all coaches just the same.

What does it really mean to be a coach? Coaching is defined as "a person who enables the athlete to achieve levels of performance to a degree that may not have been possible if left to his/her own endeavors." In order to accomplish this, coaches need to: know how to communicate to a wide variety of personalities; understand training principles; understand learning principles; have knowledge of safety issues; understand the physical requirements for the athletes; and know how to set up an evaluation system, legal issues, etc. These skills are important because coaches are asked to perform the following roles:

| | |
|---|---|
| Source of Knowledge | Motivator |
| Instructor | Strategist |
| Demonstrator | Planner |
| Evaluator | Supporter |
| Fact Finder | Spokesperson |
| Facilitator | Protector |
| Adviser | and several others |
| Mentor | |

To coach a team, an individual needs to not only understand the game but be able to communicate that knowledge to the players, motivate and encourage them to succeed and develop a strategy for success. It is a vast and multifaceted role. Coaching is part science and part art. Many aspects of coaching are based on research and scientific knowledge. However, the manner in which that knowledge is applied (e.g. how to adjust to an opponent) is more of an art. Most coaches within a specific sport use similar plays and training techniques, but do they get the same results? Why not?

The science of coaching is gathering new data and information. Much of this comes through scouting the competition. Just as generals consider the strengths and weaknesses of the opposition when preparing for battle, coaches use scouting reports to alter training or change the lineup used for the upcoming game.

The art of coaching is seen in how the information is gathered and evaluated. Each coach has his own system of review and interpretation of the information. Then the fun begins. How do we adjust to the information? Or do we ignore the information?

---

**"We work the way we practice."**
**Rick Powers, Administrator,**
**Division of Compliance, City of Indianapolis**

---

## Managers as Coaches

For managers to create a team environment in their organization, they need to be able to coach teams. They also need to understand that they will have a variety of teams to coach. The type of team will vary depending on the task/project that needs to be accomplished. But like a coach, managers will need the following skills: communicating to a wide variety of personalities, understanding training principles, understanding learning principles, knowledge of safety issues, understanding the physical requirements for their employees, how to set up tracking systems, etc. And just like a coach, managers will need to perform the following skills:

| | |
|---|---|
| Source of Knowledge | Motivator |
| Instructor | Strategist |
| Demonstrator | Planner |
| Evaluator | Supporter |
| Fact Finder | Spokesperson |
| Facilitator | Protector |
| Adviser | and several others |
| Mentor | |

Just like coaching a sports team, managing an organizational team is part science and part art. Managers will need to scout, or benchmark their competition, the market and their clients. They will also need to gather information on how their teams, departments and organization are meeting the needs of their clients. How is the product holding up in the market-place? Are clients returning for more business, or have they been stolen by the competition?

Then the manager will need to strategically communicate, plan, develop and implement changes based on the current in-formation. This is part of the art of using employees and teams to succeed.

Coaching seems like a pretty daunting task, doesn't it? Not to worry, because even on sporting teams, the coach doesn't do it all. Let's take a moment to look at the support that coaches use to build successful teams.


**The Coaching Team**

As you have learned, coaching is a very demanding position. Being able to master all the skills necessary (to not only know all the information but continue to learn, develop and imple-ment in top form) can be more than one individual can handle. So the coach develops a staff to support him—a coaching team. Depending on the type and size of the team, several assistants are needed to focus on all aspects of the team's performance.

For example, a professional football team head coach may have the following coaching staff:

| | |
|---|---|
| Offensive Coordinator | Linebacker Coach |
| Defensive Coordinator | Special Team Coach |
| Quarterback Coach | Defensive Quality Coach |
| Receivers Coach | Offensive Quality Coach |
| Tight End Coach | Defensive Backs Coach |
| Running Backs Coach | Strength and Conditioning Coach |
| Offensive Line Coach | Assistant Strength Coach |

On a football team, each of these coaches focuses on a spe-cific skill and the players who execute each role so they can be their very best. Not every team needs this level of coaching. A professional basketball team's head coach, for example, may only has about five assistant coaches and three strength and conditioning trainers/coaches.

So why do football teams need more coaches than basketball teams? The answer lies in the team itself. On a football team, players have very specific skills. The quarterback doesn't play on the defensive line. Nor does a tackle pass the football. To effectively and efficiently develop players for success, the players are separated and coached on their specific skills. It would be a total waste of time for most players to sit and wait their turn while the coach worked only with the special teams.

On a basketball team, however, all players shoot the ball, play defense and are involved in the offense. The major difference is what area of the floor they cover and their part in the plays. But they need to be more flexible during the game. They may need to switch roles and improvise.

Athletic teams also have strength and conditioning specialists to work on each player's physical status. They will tailor a development plan to build physical strength and stamina. This also includes a medical staff to treat injuries and sicknesses.

But that isn't all the support the coach has. There are whole organizations created to support these teams. These organizations usually have public relations staff, community relations staff, marketing staff, facilities/housekeeping staff, finance staff, sales staff, equipment staff, legal staff and administration. Every professional team has an entire corporation established to help them become champions.

### The Manager's Team

As the manager (now the coach), you need to rally your team. So what support do you have? In organizations, there are many people to help you coach this team. Managers have assistants or supervisors to help them develop the technical competence of the staff. Generally, managers don't have as many assistants as even a basketball coach, but that is not the only support available. But that is also where it gets a little difficult.

The various departments mentioned above that support professional sports teams are also located in most companies. The difference may lie in the diversity of needs these support structures are trying to meet. For example, your organization probably has a department to deal with marketing, but its focus is on all the needs of the organization, not just your team's.

So as the coach, you will need to be the spokesperson for the team and coordinate your efforts with the various components of your organization. It may require you to bring in resources from outside the organization. Many teams will bring in experts to provide the team support. This could include trainers, consultants or facilitators.

Review the roles of a coach and then line up the support necessary before you launch your team. Do you have the necessary support for success?

## Developing an Athletic Team

Every athletic team has a different system for planning, practice and development. For our purposes, I will use a high school football team, on which each player has a particular task to accomplish. Each focuses on his position on the team to prepare for the game. But each is also scanning the field during the play to look for opportunities. Is the defensive end in the position to grab a fumble or interception?

Creating and maintaining effective teams is an ongoing process. Regardless of whether your team is an ongoing work team or a project team, the process is the same. Let's start by examining how a high school football team plans, develops and plays the game.

We'll begin at the end of the season, when the coach meets with his staff and players to evaluate their year. What were they able to accomplish? Where did they miss the mark?

They then begin to think about next year. What are their goals? These goals, of course, include winning the championship but also include other goals like holding the opponent to a minimum number of yards or points or percentage of passes completed, etc. The players begin to set goals for their next year. These goals will then be expanded to include off-season plans and activities.

This session is followed by two sessions with just the coaching staff to finalize their plan. These sessions also include discussion of personnel issues (who plays what positions, which players are leaving, where the current weaknesses are, etc.). The coaches then meet with each player individually to discuss his goals and plans for the off season. There will be ongoing mentoring (with either the coach or a member of the coaching staff) during the off season to support the players.

The coaching staff also attends various seminars and clinics to continue learning about the newest techniques and skill development. In general, each member of the coaching staff attends at least three of these seminars (most of which are paid for by the coaching staff member themselves rather than the high school).

There are routine meetings between the coach and his staff during the off season. These meetings are used to check progress, fine tune the plan and integrate new information gathered from the various clinics. There will be sessions on integrating and developing conditioning, mental attitude and business skills. These sessions are conducted one-on-one as well as with the whole coaching staff.

The players, meanwhile, are working on personal development. This generally includes strength training and conditioning. They also attend camps to work on the skills that pertain to their specific roles on the team. These camps also are paid for by the individual, not the high school in most cases.

Before the team takes the field to compete against another team, they have preseason practices. In high school athletics, this is an intensive three-week period. During the first week, the team practices twice daily for two and half hours each. During the second and third weeks, the athletes are usually in school, so practices are reduced to once daily for two to three hours.

Before taking the practice field, there is a mandatory meeting to discuss the session. Each player must focus on an objective for that practice, which is verified by the coaching staff. Also, each player has a mentor player who is there to provide feedback during the practice.

All sessions are taped and evaluated by the coaching staff. Adjustments are made at every practice, based on individual and team performances.

During the season, the structure of the development and support changes, but an average weekly schedule might look like this:

| Friday | Game |
|---|---|
| Saturday morning | • evaluate of Friday game tapes by coaches and players<br><br>• conditioning |
| Saturday afternoon | Coaching staff only, meet for 2-3 hours to plan |
| Sunday afternoon | Coaching staff meets to review tapes of the upcoming team and make adjustment in the plan |
| Monday through Thursday | • Mandatory meeting to discuss the practice<br><br>• Set goal for practice (individual)<br><br>• Two to three hour practice |

This schedule continues throughout the season. Then the process begins again.

"See, this isn't so hard ... now who
wants to be the team mascot?"

### Developing an Organizational Team

It sounds like coaches and players eat, sleep and breathe football, doesn't it? I am sure that during the season, it probably feels that way to them and their families. But they do have other lives, which is why I have used high school football as an example. The coaching staff may consist of teachers or those who have other full-time jobs (some of these coaching positions do not pay a salary). The players are full-time students. Football may become a full-time job for a select few, but most are studying for a career. Some even have part-time jobs to go along with school and football.

This is much like being on a team at the office. Being a member of the team is only a portion of the manager's or staff's workload. So ensuring that the team's project is not only essential for the organization but also conducted in an effective manner should be a primary consideration.

Planning for the team's effort is best begun by using a tool referred to as a team charter.

## Team Charter

I am often asked, "Who should be on the team?" "How many should be on the team?" "What about the personality of the people on the team?" "Do we only want *team* players on the team?"

The answer is very simple. You need the people who have the expertise to address and solve the problems at hand. If the problem is dealing with financial issues, then you need all of your financial experts on the team as well as some end users of the information. If it is a computer issue, then you need your technical experts and, again, the users of the information.

No matter who is on the team, you must clearly identify the goals, roles and your expectations of this team. I have a team charter format that I have used to make sure that everyone is clear about what is expected.

### #1 Team Focus

In this section, you need to identify the area that the team will be targeting. Will it be an organization-wide system? Or are you looking at a specific piece of a process?

This will help your team focus on what you want them to focus on. Many times, teams get off on tangents, because that's where they think they need to go. They may have experience with the problem that has been identified and know how it affects them; however, what they end up with may not even come close to where you were hoping they would go.

For example, while working for one organization, I was asked to put together a short-term team to look at the coding process (how the employees got paid). After the meeting, I needed to clarify what was meant by the coding process. In most employees' minds, the coding process ran from when they wrote down their activities to when they received their checks. This process spanned multiple departments not to mention multiple offices within our own department. I was quickly told, however, that they were only looking at the stage of the process in which the employee was involved. That was the only function over which the department had complete control. If I had not asked for that clarification, the staff involved in the team could have very quickly focused on issues pertaining to how other departments processed the paperwork. Their time would have been wasted, they would have been frustrated, and they would have felt that management was, once again, not listening to their ideas. The employees may not have understood that it wasn't the fact that management wouldn't listen to their ideas but that any suggestions dealing with other departments were outside their control.

So giving the team the correct focus is very important. That's not to say that you tell them what you want as the end result. But you may give them some ideas as far as what you think a potential answer might be or maybe some constraints (budget, hiring, etc.) that affect the result

### #2 Why is this being studied?

In this section, you need to be clear not only with the team but with yourself. Why is it important for them to spend their time working on this project? What is the problem in the organization that you are trying to fix? What is the potential gain for the organization once it is fixed? What is the gain (and the sacrifice) for the individual team members?

The more clearly you can identify why a team is needed—while answering the question "What's in it for me?" for the employees and the organization—the better your chances of having commitment from the team members. If this is a situation in which there are some benefits but no major long-term ones, the team may not be motivated. But if this project is seen as a major effort that will have a huge impact on both them and the organization, you'll have not only their attention but their passion.

### #3 What is the goal?

Next, you must clarify the team goal. This needs to be specific and identify exactly what the limits of the team are. Are they actually going to make the decision and help implement the solution? Or are they simply making a recommendation to a management team?

You must also identify areas over which the team has no control. For example, a team looking into computer issues may be able to look at software and processes but not recommend a new computer system. The team needs to understand where their boundaries are before they start the process.

You must be very clear on whether or not you plan on implementing this recommendation if it is accepted. Having teams work on projects that you do not intend to implement, no matter what the solution, only sets you up for failure with future teams. No one wants to work on an effort that is clearly identified as having no success. There may be a possible stigma associated with being on a team like this.

### #4 What are the resources available to the team?

I think it's safe to say that team members already have full-time positions. Therefore, the work involved in being on a team is usually seen as an extra duty to most of them. They can very easily feel overwhelmed and overworked. Some people will shut down under those situations.

So ascertain what resources they might need. For example, do they need clerical support? Do they need an outside facilitator to help them keep focused? Do they need someone to help with data entry? These are only a few possibilities of what your team could need. Be sure to ask at the beginning as well as often during the process. As the team progresses, their needs may very well change.

In some cases, especially if the project is high priority, is highly visible or involves executive management with staff, an outside facilitator is recommended. (See #7 Who is on the team?)

### #5 What is the priority of the projects?

In the grand scheme of work, what is the priority of this particular project? Is it more important than other projects they are working on? How does it rank in importance with their regular job duties? If the team is not successful in completing the project, what will be the effect on the organization?

These are all very important questions to ask yourself as you're putting together your team. The team also needs this clarity. It will help them as they juggle their various job duties and team activities.

### #6 When is the project to be completed?

Knowing when a project is to be completed is crucial to assisting the team in the completion of their project. Projects with no deadlines have a tendency to go along forever. At some point, these projects become back-burner items that get little to no attention. Then the team becomes very frustrated, because they are not having success. The team slowly disappears. Deadlines give them an end to shoot for as well as a sense of urgency. It will also help them see that this is not a lifelong commitment.

### #7 Who is on the team?

This section simply identifies the names of the individuals who will be serving on the team. In some cases, it would be helpful to also list important information like the department they work in as well as phone numbers, e-mail addresses, expertise, etc.

This list should also identify who has key positions on the team. For example, the team leader is the person who is responsible for reporting to management the successes or issues the team has encountered. The lists may also include any resource people such as secretaries, technical experts, vendors or consultants.

## TEAM CHARTER

Team Focus:

Why is it being studied?

What is the goal of the team?

What resources are available to the team?

What is the priority of this project?

When is the project to be completed?

## TEAM

Team Member: _____

Team Facilitator: _____

## EXPECTATIONS

Team Facilitator:

Team Members:

Management:

I understand and agree to the above expectations:

_____     _____
Team Member                                              Date

I agree to support the above project by making time and resources available.

_____     _____
Supervisor                                              Date

On the team charter format, I have listed a team facilitator. This is not to be confused with the team leader. The facilitator is responsible for making sure the team stays on target. He or she focuses on how the team is progressing and works very closely with the leader to ensure effective team activities. In some cases, the team facilitator could be another staff person. In situations where the team is working on very complex or controversial projects, it may benefit the organization to bring in a consultant to facilitate the activity. The facilitator should be a completely unbiased individual. His only focus is making sure the team has effectively researched, analyzed and developed a solution.

As your team environment develops, the facilitator duties could become the duties of the team leader. Or the facilitator duties could be rotated among the team members.

*A word of caution: Facilitating a team takes training and practice. The use of a professional facilitator will provide the team with someone who can assist them in reaching their goals.*

### #8 Expectations

The expectations section identifies exactly what you want each role on the team to accomplish. This will give the team clarity as to who is responsible for certain support tasks. How many times have you been on a team where things have fallen through the cracks? By clearly identifying the expectations, you begin to get past obstacles; this clarifies responsibilities not just between you and the team but also between the team members.

Here is an example of the expectation of the team facilitator:

## *Facilitator:*

- Focus of how the team is getting the work completed
- Assist the team in breaking down the project
- Work with team leader to plan from upcoming meetings
- Train team in the tools necessary to perform their tasks
- Help the team prepare for presentations

### *#9 Signatures*

The signatures are used to ensure that both members and their immediate managers alike understand the commitment to the project. By signing the document, the members now have a vested interest in the project because they have signed onto it.

### Preseason Practice

As you have read the different parts of this team charter, it may seem as though only the creator of the team has input. Before the team begins their work, however, there should be a meeting between the team leader, the team champion* and the team facilitator to discuss the charter. The team then reviews, makes suggestions about and approves the charter.

---

**\*Team Champion—**Is usually an individual in an executive position that is interested in the success of the team. This individual can intercede for the team to help get past obstacles that may occur between units in the organization.

---

This will also offer them the opportunity to ask for clarification of your thoughts. What you wrote may be clear to you, but that doesn't guarantee that it is to everyone else. The team needs to totally understand what is expected and asked of them. They then need to take this agreement to their supervisors, who must also agree to have their employees involved in this effort.

I know that having a supervisor sign this document seems a little bureaucratic, but I have seen many teams fail because certain key members were not allowed to fully participate in the team due to their supervisors' pressure. This gives the supervisors the opportunity to fully understand what is expected of their employees and the time needed to reach their goal. Supervisors can then discuss with management their concerns and issues about the employees accomplishing their normal duties. Do they need additional support staff to cover for their participating team members?

## The Season

Throughout the project, the team leader and facilitator should be constantly monitoring the team's progress. This should also involve the team's assessment of how they feel about the process. These evaluations could be simple plus and minus ratings given after each session, or they could take the form of a more formalized survey and evaluation.

The results of these evaluations should be discussed with the team. The information should be used to develop activities to help them work more effectively. Remedial activities could be skill development, a retreat or identifying additional resources.

The team leader and facilitator should regularly meet with the team champion to ensure that the team is on track. This also allows for the champion to fill the leader and facilitator in on any other updates or information that may be necessary for the team's success. This could include organizational changes, product changes, etc.

**End of Project**

Once the team has finished their project, a celebration event should be arranged. This should occur no matter what the results (even if the team's recommendation cannot be implemented). The purpose of this event is to:

- Celebrate finishing the project
- Identifying lessons learned
- Identify ways to be more effective with next effort

Many times, teams believe their efforts go unrecognized by the organization, especially if their recommendations are not accepted, so the end-of-the-project celebration should include a discussion of status of the team's efforts. Was the team's recommendation accepted? If not, why not? If it was, what are the next steps?

**Conclusion**

Teams can be a powerful force for your organization. Therefore, they should be used only when the organization truly supports the activity. Continuing to commission teams and let them flounder does more damage than good. This is not to say that an organization can't have multiple teams. Just as one individual can effectively manage a limited number of people, an organization can effectively manage a number of teams.

How many teams should be used and at what levels are your decisions to make. By properly planning and supporting the commissioned teams, your organization will be able to reap many benefits. The more successful your teams are, the more likely future teams will also be successful. Also, the more successful your teams are, the more motivated your employees will be to participate in the team's efforts.

**Teamwork is hard, but it is also very energizing and extremely rewarding. Use your teams wisely!**

## About The Author

## Margie Thomas, CTC

 What do you get when you spell Chaos? Margie Thomas! Margie works with organizations to tame the chaos that can inhibit productivity. Margie brings to her clientele: **C— Creativity, H—Hands-On Skills, A—Analytical Process, O—Optimizer, S—Solution-Oriented Outcomes**.

As President of M.A.T. Consulting, Margie combines her 12 years experience training and facilitating with her 15 years management experience to help organizations learn how to tame the chaos. Drawing from her scientific degrees in Biology and Chemistry from Indiana University, she has studied the complex elements that make organizations thrive. Through her personalized strategic process, Margie offers her clients specific tools and techniques to enhance leadership skills and job performances. Clients of M.A.T. Consulting have included corporations, government agencies, small business owners, and non-profit entities. Whether working with individuals or teams of employees, Margie offers her cost effective methods to benefit the bottom line. Specific areas of training include: *Time Management, Stress Management, Conflict Resolution, Leadership Training, Personality Inventory, Project Management, Team Development, and Customer Service.*

Professional memberships include the National Speakers Association, International Association of Facilitators, Association of Psychological Type, Zonta International and Central Indiana Association for Training and Development.

Margie Thomas, CTC
Productivity Strategist™
M.A.T. Consulting, Inc.
4080 E 750 N
Lebanon, IN  46052
(765)325-2482
(530)453-2990 – fax
margie@matconsulting.com
www.matconsulting.com

# Chapter Four

## Teambuilding is Everyone's Business

### Terry Wall, CMC

**Why a book on teambuilding?**

One reason is that teambuilding is everyone's business—directors, managers and employees alike. Most people would agree that teams generally accomplish more than individuals because of synergy—the interaction of two or more forces whose combined impact is much greater than their individual effects. This is why we see such an emphasis on teamwork in today's business world. So if you want to be effective in your workplace at any given level, you need to know something about teambuilding and how to be an effective team member.

Another reason for this book is that teamwork is essential to almost all the other topics in the PowerLearning series, whether it's leadership, customer service, management theory, success, diversity or career planning. The teambuilding concept is also relevant to just about any topic in the business world today, from emotional intelligence to mergers and acquisitions, because your effectiveness in these areas will depend on your ability to build strong teams and your skill at working within a team environment.

The constantly changing nature of organizations is yet another reason that teambuilding is an essential skill. Within corporations, small businesses and even nonprofit organizations, one central theme is dominant in the 21st century: Fierce competition is forcing organizations to do more with less, to increase productivity with fewer employees, fewer managers and fewer support people. Adding to such pressures is a growing scarcity of natural, material and human resources, which requires downsizing, rightsizing or tightsizing. And when you're trying to achieve more with fewer people, teamwork becomes indispensable. The organizations that can't build successful teams, and the individuals who lack teambuilding skills, are at a clear disadvantage.

Research by Dr. David Swenson, management professor at The College Of Saint Scholastica in Duluth, Minnesota, indicates that the following gains were the result of an emphasis on teambuilding:

- Shenandoah Life decreased its case-handling time from twenty-seven days to just two.

- Sherwin-Williams lowered costs by forty-five percent and reduced returned goods by seventy-five percent.

- Tavistock Coal increased output by twenty-five percent and reduced absenteeism by seventy-five percent.

- Proctor & Gamble reduced manufacturing costs by thirty to fifty percent.

- Kodak improved SPC by 228 percent, safety by sixty-seven percent, output by twelve percent and decreased costs by eleven percent.

- GE improved productivity by 250 percent.

- Westinghouse reduced cycle time from seventeen days to just seven.

- Ford lowered its defect rate below that of most Japanese competitors.

- General Mills's productivity in team-oriented plants was twenty percent better than in its traditional plants.
- American Transtech reduced both costs and processing time by fifty percent.
- Kimball Manufacturing in Boise, Idaho, reduced production time by fifty percent and work-in-process inventory from fourteen to three and a half days.

A study of self-directed work teams in seven countries reveals that ninety-three percent increased productivity, eighty-six percent lowered operating costs, eighty-six percent enhanced quality, and seventy percent improved employee attitudes.

Just how prevalent is the use of teams today? *Industry Week* reported that sixty-eight percent of small companies are using teams and that within such companies, twenty-five to ninety-nine percent of their employees work in teams. It certainly looks as if teams are here to stay in the business world.

Additionally, teambuilding is a skill that applies in almost any setting. For instance, we often think of teams as having official designations: a cross-functional work team, a self-directed team, an ad hoc team or even a project committee. But when you think about it, we also work in a lot of *unofficial* teams that require teamwork and teambuilding skills. For example, a group of people working on a particular line on the shop floor is a team. Any department or division within an organization, whether it's a corporation or a nonprofit, is a team. The organization itself is a team, composed of several smaller teams. You should therefore become accustomed to thinking in terms of the many applications of teambuilding concepts.

A final reason for this book is that outside the workplace, we also find ourselves working in teams, even though we might not have thought of them as such. Are you active in your church? That in itself can be thought of as a team, and the local unit of that organization is often broken down into various committees or ministries, all of which can be considered teams. Do you belong to a neighborhood or community association, a civic group, social club, volunteer organization, the Boy Scouts or Girl Scouts? Again, all are teams. Then there is the first team we all encounter—the family. And let's not overlook the primary team that creates the family—a marriage. When you think about it, teams have been the foundation for getting things done since that very first team of Adam and Eve.

Those of you who have children or who might be students or teachers should also keep in mind that the educational setting involves a whole host of teams. We know that schools have sports teams, chess teams, debate teams and various clubs, but beyond these obvious examples, each group of students constitutes a team. For instance, an individual classroom full of students is a team, and all the classes together form a team— the eighth grade, the senior class, the college school of engineering and so on. And all those grades or departments form one big team, which is the school as a whole.

Obviously, teams are everywhere. We simply cannot avoid them or being a part of them, which is why I like to say, "Teambuilding really is everyone's business." And if we want to be effective team members, we must also be effective team builders. In this light, then, the information in this and subsequent chapters will help you build the team you need to be most effective.

By the way, you don't have to be a team leader to use the teambuilding strategies found in this book. In training or facilitation sessions I conduct with organizations, I tell people, "You are the CEO of your job, of your part of the organization, and therefore, you must take personal responsibility for doing that job." (This surprises most people—unless they really are CEOs!) I say this whether I'm working with division heads, plant managers or front-line employees, because I truly believe that each individual should hold himself or herself accountable for getting results on the job. I'll paraphrase that idea here by saying, "You are the team leader for your job on the team." Even if you're not the official team leader, you can at least take responsibility for your contribution to the team and even for the contributions of those team members you might influence.

In that sense, you can use the strategies in this book to improve teambuilding in the others around you.

Yes, teambuilding *is* everyone's business, so let's get started.

## What is a Team?

I believe simple is better, so I use a definition from Ken Ross, who is Senior Manager of Media Relations at Lockheed Martin's facility in Moorestown, New Jersey. His definition isn't fancy and doesn't require a Ph.D. in linguistics: "A team is a group of people who are focused on the same goals, who work together well, and who are committed to achieving results."

## Know Yourself

One essential teambuilding skill involves knowing yourself. This skill really has two components: knowing what motivates you, and finding your passion. If you know how to motivate yourself, you can stay sharp and competitive. And if you discover your passion, your enthusiasm and commitment become contagious, lifting other team members to new heights and enabling them to accomplish more. Your passion can be the fuse that sparks the explosion of creativity and commitment that powers the engine of achievement.

Knowing yourself is simple enough. You need to take a hard look at what you've done, what you are able to do right now and what you want to accomplish in the future. Then you need to gather input from others. (Later we'll discuss one way to do that—an exercise called The Hot Seat. This is simply a way to get honest feedback from your peers, and although it must be done in a controlled environment, it produces valuable results.) You can gather important feedback through 360-degree appraisals (getting others to rate you on a predetermined set of criteria) or through self-scoring learning instruments, such as DiSC products from Inscape Publishing (not to be confused with Insight Publishing, the publisher of this book). These products can give you tremendous amounts of insight into yourself and how you can be more effective in teambuilding.

The passion part comes simply from looking at what you have done, are doing, and want to do, and seeing what you really get excited about. Once you identify that, you can try to structure your team and environment so that you are doing the things that excite you, because your passion can be contagious.

And remember that you don't have to be the team leader to do these things. You can always run ideas by the team leader, but ultimately you are responsible for motivating yourself and others, no matter what your official title is. The important thing is recognizing that you are in control, and that you must take steps to ensure that results are achieved. You are the CEO of your job, and you are the team leader for yourself and your own contribution to the team.

## The Role of the Individual

Let me address something you might not expect in a book on teambuilding—the individual. I recently came across a book, *The Wisdom of Teams*, that reminded me of one of the great myths about teams: All you have to do is get a bunch of people together, call them a team and wait for the glorious results to come streaming in. The truth is that building successful teams is never that easy. I believe that many teambuilding efforts fail because we are so focused on the team that we forget about individuals. But you see, a team is a collection of individuals. As a leader, or even as a team member, you must always start with individuals when trying to improve team performance. You might call this approach The Wisdom of One.

Why emphasize the individual in a book about teambuilding? Because individuals are the building blocks of a team, and ignoring the individual is like ignoring the individual bricks in masonry construction, or the individual links in a chain. The best way to build an effective team is to start with individuals, one at a time. Unless you focus on each individual and remember that each one brings certain characteristics, strengths and weaknesses to the group, your team is much less likely to succeed.

All too often, however, people try to create teams without realizing that real motivation and skill come from the individual. Just as you can't just slap any types of brick together in a masonry project, you can't accept just any individuals for a team, no matter how impressive their technical credentials. That's why, when putting together a team, the true leader first looks at the individuals who would comprise it. Consider how one wrong selection can wreak havoc on a team's performance. Show me an individual who isn't self motivated, isn't prone to cooperate, isn't likely to share information freely or lend a hand to a colleague without any hope of receiving credit, and I'll show you a person who will drag team performance down.

As I said earlier, one reason that the team concept is so widespread has to do with synergy—the interaction of two or more forces whose combined impact is greater than their individual effects. But there can also be negative synergy—poor individual performance that has a greater adverse effect in a team environment than it would in isolation. This negative synergy drags down not only an individual's productivity, but also the effectiveness of coworkers.

## Strategies for Moving From Individuals to Teams

To build more effective teams, take the following steps, all of which are focused on the individual.

- Define specifically the reason for putting together the team, because this tells you what to look for in individuals. Is the goal to increase sales? Improve customer satisfaction ratings? Develop new ideas or processes for the factory floor? These purposes require different skills. Also consider how (and how often) the team will meet. A team that meets face to face doesn't require the self-discipline that might be necessary for a "virtual team" that meets electronically. And a team that meets daily operates differently and has different expectations of team members than one that meets infrequently but expects team members to be self-managing, working on individual tasks and sharing information between team meetings.

- Determine the specific traits needed for success in meeting team goals. Although you are looking at individual skills, you must also consider how a given skill fits into the team component. For instance, if the team must produce written reports and you select one individual because of strong writing skills, you will be doing the team a disservice if that person is not thick-skinned enough to accept constructive feedback from other team members. You need someone who not only has good writing skills, but also is not overly sensitive to criticism.

- Screen your candidates to find individuals who possess the traits you desire. Understand how your prospective team members really work and what their true habits and drives are. Don't just accept what they claim about themselves.

Here's a way to screen for team membership: Even though you are focusing on the individual when putting together the team, base your decision not just on an interview with the individual but on a trial-run group activity. For instance, say you are looking for four or five people for a team. Provide eight or so potential candidates with a group task and observe individual behaviors as they carry it out. This will give you true insight into to how the individuals might perform in a team setting. Base your selection on how well the individuals perform in a group setting, and be just as selective as if you were making a real hiring decision. Remember that although the candidates are already employees, you are in effect "hiring" them to be part of a team. (You can also use this strategy when hiring new employees if your hiring is part of an overall team-building process.)

- Assemble the team and tell them their goals. Encourage the individuals selected to identify specific goals that relate to any team goals. (This provides greater clarity and appeals to individual motivation, which is essential for team success.)

- Evaluate performance, but don't forget to evaluate individual as well as team performance. To maximize team effectiveness, you must look at each individual's performance, because individual motivation, skills and abilities are the building blocks of team performance. So just as you focus on the individual at the beginning of the team process, also focus on the individual in the evaluation process. By evaluating team performance only, you miss the opportunity to improve individual performance. And improving individual performance increases synergy and overall team results. Consider having members assess the performances of their teammates; they know best who contributed what.

The bottom line: In order to maximize team performance, you must focus on the individual when selecting, coaching, and evaluating a team. Remember that you must seek out The Wisdom of One before reaping the benefits of The Wisdom of Teams.

## Working With an Existing Team

What about the intact team? How can you make it more effective? The first key is to know your players as well as their strengths and weaknesses. Again, this applies whether or not you are the team leader. Remember that you are responsible for your own contribution to the team, and just as you need to know yourself first, your next step is to know your team members. You do this by not being so narrowly focused on your own contribution that you miss important aspects of other members' strengths and weaknesses. Once you know those, you will be better able to assess which members are best suited for certain tasks. Also, you can then help those individuals make needed improvements in certain skills.

What if you are the team leader? One of the best exercises I know for getting to know team members' strengths and weaknesses is also a good exercise for clearing the air, getting unspoken topics out in the open, and building a sense of team trust. I call it The Hot Seat. It works like this:

Let's say you have a ten-member team. Acting as the facilitator, give each member a sheet of paper that has five columns. In the first column, ask everyone to write down the names of all the other team members. The remaining four columns have the following headings: Strengths, Suggestions for Improvement, Things I Can Provide to That Team Member, and Things I Need From That Team Member. Instruct everyone to write for each team member a maximum of two items per column. Limiting it to two items per column prevents people from writing a book about each item (areas of improvement, for instance). When they're done, everyone should have identified specific but brief items for each of the other team members.

Then explain that each team member will take a turn on "the hot seat." While Person Number One is on the hot seat, Person Number Two, speaking directly to Person Number One, tells what he or she has written about Person Number One, who is allowed to take notes but make no response. Then Person Number Three goes over his or her list for Person Number One. Then Person Number Four, and so on. After all have had their say, Person Number One can give a brief (no more than a minute or two) response—not a rebuttal or defense but simply a reaction to the information received from the rest of the team (e.g. "I knew I had a short temper, but I didn't know that people appreciate my sense of humor").

Next, Person Number Two takes the hot seat, and one by one, the other members of the team tell that person what they have written. At the end of that round, Person Number Two gets to give a brief reaction (again, not a rebuttal or defense). Then it's Person Number Three's turn and so on.

## *A couple thoughts on conducting this exercise:*

First, one of my guiding principles when facilitating team-building sessions is that I don't force people to do anything. So I always allow those who feel uncomfortable during this exercise the option of passing on any particular individual. If Person Number Five, for example, doesn't want to address Person Number Seven, for whatever reason, or does not even want to take a turn on the hot seat, that's fine. If a facilitator establishes trust early on, though, this usually isn't a problem. Still, some people may not want to participate, and that's okay. Other times, particularly with people who may know each other in only a casual way, some team members may not feel qualified to comment on certain areas. That's okay, too, but I've found that the vast majority will participate.

Second, you'll find that not everyone will have two things to list in each column and that some people won't have any. Again, this is usually because one person doesn't know the other well enough or because he or she doesn't feel comfortable providing that information. That's fine, too, because we don't force people to participate.

I've conducted this exercise in many different settings—in manufacturing and service industries, with supervisors and front-line employees, in corporations and non-profits. As a facilitator, I've usually been able to establish a high level of trust among the team members themselves and convince everyone that as an objective outsider, I will not let things get out of hand.

How do you establish a basis for such trust? At the beginning of any teambuilding session, I always establish four rules:

1. You should try to participate in some way.

2. What you hear about other team members (and about others not present during the session) won't leave the room.

3. You should treat each other (especially during the Hot Seat exercise) with dignity and respect; no cheap shots.

4. "Look in the mirror first." In other words, when you hear about a particular skill or behavior, don't think, "Yeah, Joe

should really take Terry's advice about treating people with dignity and respect." Instead, look in the mirror first and ask, "How does this relate to *me*? How can *I* do better at treating people with dignity and respect?" Only after looking in the mirror first can you consider how the concept or skill might apply to others.

So before the Hot Seat exercise, I remind everyone of these rules (with particular emphasis on treating others with dignity and respect), and elicit from the group a commitment to follow these guidelines. Because of this trust, this exercise is always constructive, and having conducted it for several years in many different settings, I've never had a bad experience with it.

That doesn't mean there haven't been some tense moments, or that some people haven't needed to step back and calm down; that has happened a few times. But the experience has always been constructive.

This exercise has many benefits. The most obvious is that team members develop insight into their own strengths and weaknesses. They also have a better sense of the strengths and weaknesses of other members. The value of the resulting trust (another benefit) is almost immeasurable. This trust develops because in such a controlled setting, team members see that they can confront others about sensitive issues without being destructive, and that they can accept constructive feedback without ill will. Participants also learn the value of resolving conflict effectively rather than merely suppressing topics that need airing.

This exercise develops other important communication skills as well. For instance, I remind team members to speak directly to the person on the hot seat. I emphasize this repeatedly, because the tendency is to address me as the facilitator or the other team members—anything to avoid looking directly at the person on the hot seat. Most times, we associate such reluctance with giving negative information, but I find that people also hesitate to look directly at others when relating their strengths.

Which brings me to another benefit of The Hot Seat exercise: It teaches team members the importance of giving positive feedback. In fact, I have seen some people become emotionally moved upon receiving it. The person on the hot seat often says that he or she never knew that the other team members really appreciated his or her strengths. Finally, they learn that giving positive feedback is important not just in this exercise, but on an ongoing basis.

## Customer Service as a Part of Teambuilding

Some people don't recognize the importance of customer service in a team environment, but it is very important, especially if team members are from different departments. In these situations, team members often are so focused on the external customer or on departmental loyalties that they neglect team loyalty. The trick is to get them to regard other team members as internal customers, and to focus on doing what's best for the team (provided, of course, that the team's goals are aligned with organizational goals or what's best for the organization as a whole).

One of the best examples that I have seen of this took place at Durand Glass Manufacturing Company in Millville, New Jersey, makers of a variety of high-quality glass products (drinking glasses, wine glasses, plates, etc.). In 1999, I was doing a needs assessment to determine how their management team could work together more effectively, when I noticed that all of the departments—in fact, all 1,000 employees—were focused on the external customers. The people who bought glassware at department stores were one set of customers, but Durand employees also regarded the department stores as customers. When doing the needs assessment, I frequently heard people mention the customer. "We've got to get this job out today or it won't get to the customer on time" or "We've got to use different packing material or the customer will open the box only to find damaged glass." I was impressed with this attitude and thought that if the departments within the plant had the same concern for their internal customers, the entire plant

91

would operate more smoothly. Of course, this idea needed to be adopted by the management team I was working with—the department heads.

I discussed this with the plant manager, Glen Halter, and explained that department heads needed to regard other departments as internal customers and focus on their needs along with external customer needs instead of just watching out for their own departments. Glen asked how they could do this if one department (the Hot End) was sending product to another department (the Cold End), where the product was inspected for quality and then packed into boxes. He understood how the Hot End could regard the Cold End as its customer, since the Hot End was physically sending product to the Cold End. But how, he wondered, could the Cold End regard the Hot End as its customer? What product was involved?

I explained that in this instance, the product was often information, not glass. For instance, if the Hot End knew that because of a mechanical problem, defective glass was going to the Cold End, giving advance notice to the Cold End would help Cold-End employees. Going the other way, if the Cold End noticed some flaws that were probably the result of a faulty machine setting in the Hot End, and they communicated that information (the product) to the Hot End immediately, the Hot End could quickly make the proper adjustment. But the key was in recognizing that the two departments were customers of each other, and that if each treated the other department as a customer and looked at how it could best meet that customer's needs, overall teamwork would improve. So it was up to the department heads, the management team, to start regarding other department heads and their corresponding departments, as customers.

To apply this to your own teambuilding efforts, you have to ask yourself and your team members some questions. Who is the team? What are the duties and functions of other team members? What is the product I send to other team members? What product do they send to me? How can I improve in meeting that customer's (team member's) needs? Most often, the best way to find out how to meet someone's needs is to ask that person. (A lot of this comes out in the Hot Seat exercise, when talking about what team members need from each other.)

## Crucial Communication Skills

As we have seen, the ability to provide both positive feedback (communication designed to get people to repeat behavior) and constructive feedback (communication designed to get people to change behavior) is crucial in the Hot Seat exercise. Lack of these communication skills is often at the heart of many organizational problems, and nowhere is this more evident than in teambuilding. The way we communicate can be constructive or destructive. Again, it's about treating people with dignity and respect, and the simple fact is that destructive communication destroys team members' motivation, attitude and commitment. This is perhaps more important in team settings, because the success of the team depends on how well the members work together.

This is even more crucial when teams are ad hoc, cross-functional, or virtual (not located together), because the amount of interaction is less than that of teams located in the same place. When time is scarce, the fence mending that is needed to overcome destructive communication often doesn't get done. This leads to conflict, animosity and resentment, all of which can erode, if not destroy, the effectiveness of a team.

So learning that we must give positive and constructive feedback is essential to the teambuilding process; the key is to provide this communication, whether constructive or positive, on an ongoing basis. Otherwise, the unwanted behavior, not the desired behavior, will be repeated.

And remember that doing or saying nothing constitutes acceptance of a particular behavior. Think of it this way: If your eight-year-old comes home from school, and you observe him throwing his coat and books in the middle of the family room floor before going out to play, and you say nothing, what are you communicating to the child? You are in effect saying that it's okay for him to leave his coat and books in a heap in the middle of the family room. And you are increasing the likelihood that this behavior will be repeated. Saying nothing, then, is a form of positive feedback, albeit a subtle one. As someone once said, we cannot *not* communicate. Even when we're saying nothing, we're saying that the behavior in question is acceptable. By saying nothing, we're actually saying a great deal.

So if you want team members or the team as a whole to repeat a particular behavior, provide positive feedback and provide it often. If, on the other hand, you want the behavior changed, provide constructive feedback. And remember to be specific in describing the behavior as well as its effect on the team so that team members will have a clear understanding of what is expected of them.

## The Concept Of Consensus

Another important teambuilding concept to understand is consensus—the accepted way of reaching decisions in a team environment. Essentially, it means that all team members can support a decision, even though that decision might not be perfect or even the best decision in the eyes of some team members.

To effectively reach a consensus decision, you must recognize that most problems do not have a single right answer. Instead, good decisions approximate being right. You are most likely to reach a consensus decision when you step away from the view that your way is the best and only way to see the problem. Reaching consensus is even more likely when:

- Voting and majority rule are not used to defeat dissenting members.

- Priority is placed on ranking items in a way that all members can live with.

- Alternatives and rankings are modified to satisfy members with serious reservations.

- Members build upon that on which they agree, rather than focusing on areas of disagreement.

## The Composition of the Team

How you compose your team is an important consideration, one that requires what I call "diversity with understanding." We know intuitively that we don't want a team that is made up of the same kind of people, because one of the advantages of teams is the ability to provide a variety of perspectives. But another benefit of teams is that a well-composed team will have a variety of personalities as well as differing approaches to communicating (talkative versus reserved), problem-solving (analytical versus quick-thinking), and processing information (linear-thinking versus creative). Each type of individual brings strengths and weaknesses to the table, and to reap the full benefits of teams, we want to harness those strengths and diminish the weaknesses. But diversity in approach, problem-solving and so on is not enough. We also need ethnic and cultural diversity as well as people who can accept, understand and value approaches that are different. Only then does diversity become a tremendous advantage.

## Training for the Team

If for no other reason than diversity, the team concept requires training to help people identify, understand and appreciate the variety of approaches that is the hallmark of effective teams. But the necessary training must go beyond the diversity issue. The training must address why teams are important as well as the different stages of team development and crucial skills such as leadership, communications, relationship building, problem solving, conflict resolution, etc.

You also need a variety of leadership styles, not just among team members but also within team members. Even if only one person is designated as the team leader, other team members will have to display leadership qualities in a variety of situations. Team members will have to show leadership when the official leader is absent. They will need to display leadership in dealing with the team leader and with other team members.

Equally important, team members will have to display leadership in trying to work with people outside the team.

Since teams often rely on non-team members in other organizations for providing important resources and information, the ability to display leadership when interacting with others is absolutely essential. In fact, Daniel Goleman, the popular Emotional Intelligence author and researcher, has shown that the ability to obtain information through informal networks often distinguishes star performers from average and below-average performers.

The leadership key in team interactions is being able to accurately assess situations and determine and use the leadership style that is most appropriate. For instance, when I'm facilitating a teambuilding session, I often throw scenarios out to the participants and ask for their thoughts and opinions. That's when I wear my "facilitator hat." As I demonstrate, though, when the situation changes—say a fire in the back of the room—I'm not going to ask for their opinions: "How do you feel about that fire?" Instead, I'll move into a command-and-control leadership mode: "Fire! Everyone out!" This example of change in leadership style is intentionally rather stark, but you get the point. Although the differences in leadership style required in team situations are often much more subtle, we need to be skilled at displaying a variety of leadership styles on a team.

Speaking of command-and-control leadership, the person responsible for overseeing the team's work and its progress, usually a manager of some sort, needs to employ a different type of leadership in overseeing the team's activities. In this situation, the manager's role is to monitor progress and performance and offer guidance, support and resources; thus, a command-and-control style can destroy a team. This manager must recognize that command and control, in most situations, will counteract the synergy of the team (another form of negative synergy). The benefits of a team approach are more likely to be realized if this manager's leadership style promotes autonomy in decision-making and risk taking. This doesn't mean you never use command and control, because sometimes that style is warranted (underperformance of the team or some of its members, for example). Again, flexibility is the key.

As I mentioned earlier, 360-degree feedback and self-scoring instruments like DiSC are ways of finding out how you relate to other people. These can include looking at your leadership, problem-solving, conflict-resolution, and communication skills. You need to determine what skills need improvement and then improve them through training.

## Buy-In

Another key to success in any teambuilding project is the concept of buy-in—getting the important people to accept the idea that teams are essential to improvement. There are two sets of people for whom this is essential: management, including the top management team, and the employees. Keep in mind that teambuilding, and the adoption of the team concept, often requires a change in thinking of the people involved. This is because the built-in, natural resistance to change will probably express itself with a mentality of, "We do it this way, because that's the way we've always done it. So we don't see any reason to try teams." This means that you often have to transform the culture into one that embraces a more collaborative, team-oriented approach. You can usually obtain buy-in from management by presenting the extensive research statistics that show how teamwork improves overall productivity and profitability. If top management, or at least the management in your division or department, isn't 100-percent supportive of the team concept, you will have great difficulty gaining buy-in from the employees.

To obtain buy-in from the employees in a teambuilding session, you can implement a wide range of teambuilding activities that illustrate the principle of synergy. One example is the Survival Exercise: You imagine you are stranded in the desert with a group of people. Your group has a dozen or so items that may or may not be useful to your survival, and your job is to rank those items in order of importance for helping you survive. The items are ranked first individually, then as a team. Finally, team members review an expert's ranking of the items. The vast majority of teams comes closer to the right answers than do individuals working alone, but even for teams who don't, this exercise illustrates a lot of important concepts about the superiority of teams.

## Conclusion

Teambuilding is necessary because advances in technology and increases in competition require companies and organizations to produce more with higher quality while also reducing costs. Teams help you do these things.

So keep in mind that whether your team is at work or in the community, whether it's an ad hoc committee or permanent, whether it's your family, your marriage or some other personal relationship, teamwork is everyone's business.

## About The Author

### Terry Wall, CMC

Terry Wall, CMC, President of T.G. Wall Management Consulting, is a recognized expert on teambuilding, strategy, and leadership. His management and consulting experience have helped businesses and organizations increase profitability and productivity. As a professional speaker, consultant, and trainer, he works in a wide range of industries, including service and manufacturing, nonprofit, and large and small organizations. A skilled facilitator, Terry also belongs to the National Speakers Association, Toastmasters International, and the Society for Human Resource Management. He has a B.A. in Psychology from Rockhurst University in Kansas City, and an MBA from Drexel University in Philadelphia.

Terry Wall, CMC, President
T.G. Wall Management Consulting, LLC
6 Emerson Lane
Washington Township, NJ 08080
Phone: 856-218-7200
email: terry@tgwall.com
web: http://www.tgwall.com

# Chapter Five

## A Step Beyond:
## Building High-Performing Teams

### Jan Baller

Full engagement—it's the hottest area of focus in business circles right now. And these are the questions that business leaders are asking most often:

- "How do we get employees fully engaged in the success of the company?"
- "How do we get employees contributing at their highest level?"
- "How can we make everyone a player?"
- "How do we make sure everyone is 'thinking like an owner?'"
- "How can we retain people when we only have a few key positions to promote people into?"

A recent Gallup poll points out some alarming statistics. The findings are that in a data base of two million employees and 80,000 managers:

- Twenty-nine percent of the American workforce are *engaged* employees. These are employees who show consistent levels of high performance. They are the energetic, highly motivated, go-to players that you can count on every time—the employees who are committed and see themselves building the future of the organization.

- Fifty-five percent are *not engaged* (or not *as* engaged). These employees are just putting in their time as expected. They are achieving the goals they have established and doing what they need to do to keep their jobs. But they only see their work as a job and nothing more. These employees don't feel a sense of connection with their organization and where its going, or they can't fully support their organization's values or approaches. They may not feel connected to their managers or feel like a part of their work teams. This group is a "wait and see" group rather than a group of employees fully committed to building the future of the organization.

- Sixteen percent are *actively disengaged*. Actively disengaged employees don't just feel unhappy at work; they act out that unhappiness. They find it almost impossible to become part of the solution, because they thrive on being part of the problem. They are critical of the company, its leaders, its decisions, and they make their discontent known to whomever will listen.

* Research statistics from Curt Coffman, *First Break All the Rules*

How do these statistics compare to your workplace? If they ring true for your situation, *these are devastating numbers*! If you're paying everyone full salary and only getting one third of your employees contributing at their highest level, you're faced with the very critical questions above.

## High-Performing Teams are an Answer!

I believe that finding the answers to these questions lies in achieving mastery of the subject of this chapter, *Building High-Performance Teams*. We can make everyone players by involving them in teams that can make a positive difference. We may not have enough positions to promote everyone, but we can create teams and give them challenging assignments and real authority to act. It's not hard to motivate people when they know they have an important role that will make a big difference to the success of the company.

---

**High-performing teams will transform organizations from hierarchies to empowered, flexible, fully engaged organizations.**

---

When employees are involved in teams that work, they are fully engaged. Their hearts are in it, and they are thinking like owners. Creativity and ideas flow. Commitment soars when employees are given real responsibility. If the responsibility is real, teams step up and show they are ready to run with it. The major reason we have had such a great emphasis on teams in the last ten years is that this is the new organizational structure of the future. High-performing teams will transform organizations from hierarchies to empowered, flexible, fully engaged organizations.

Organizations will rely on empowered teams to meet the majority of needs that employees in the workplace have in common. Everyone has the need to be connected and have a sense of belonging. Everyone has a need for recognition and appreciation. When employees are involved in small teams, they are connected, and they are recognized and appreciated more regularly. Everyone has a need to make a positive difference. Sometimes, it's hard to know if you're making a difference when you're a tiny cog in a huge wheel. But with teams, you know you're making a difference, and it feels great.

Teams are essential in today's workplace, because problems are so complex. An individual working alone can't redesign a process. Individual perspectives are insufficient to get a grasp on the complexities we face today. We need a cross-section of people, each with different perspectives, different talents and skills, working together to address the issues that challenge us. We will achieve flexibility, speed, a focus on people, creativity, expansive knowledge and insight—everything that's important—through how successfully we build teams.

For a good example of an exemplary team-based organization that is flourishing financially and creating an amazingly positive environment for employees, do some research on the Gore company (www.gore.com), well-known creators of Gore-Tex. They describe their culture as team-based, with no hierarchy, no chains of command, no traditional titles indicating power and authority. Their organization is set up in multidisciplinary teams of associates who are organized around business objectives. Each team feels a great deal of ownership and a high-level commitment to accomplishing its objectives. The company has been selected by *Fortune* Magazine as one of the 100 Best Companies to Work for In America every year from 1998 to 2003. This year, they ranked number twelve on the list, which is a prestigious accomplishment. They are a shining example of an organization that has gone the distance in providing the maximum environment for success for all of its employees.

You can tell I'm a passionate advocate for the power and potential of teams. I've been involved with building teams for many years, and I've seen amazing changes from people who have figured out what it really takes to mature a team to its highest level of functioning. I've worked in the trenches, and I've studied the research, but mostly I've learned from walking the walk with teams through their developmental process. My clients have given me a wonderful education, and I am deeply grateful for what I've learned through working alongside them.

## My Personal Discovery of the Power and Potential of Teams

I discovered the power and the importance of teams when I was involved in a consulting contract at IBM in the early nineties. My role there was as a contract trainer, teaching classes on leadership, creativity and innovation as well as a variety of professional development classes. I got to know many of the employees very well. One day as we were having lunch together, they asked me, "What would you do if you had the job of transforming this organization from a top-down hierarchy to an empowered organization?" My first response was, "I'd build teams, train them and turn them loose on challenging assignments, with real power to act." We had an energized conversation that day, and I didn't think much more about it. But several of these employees thought a lot more about it! One day they called me and said, "Exciting news! We have been commissioned as an employee team to help transform this division into a team-based, highly empowered organization. Our mission is to take the consulting expertise that we have been providing internally to IBM, package it and take it out to the marketplace. Our goal is to generate a six-million-dollar stream of revenue in three years. Would you work with us to provide coaching and training components for our initiative?"

> **"What would you do if you had the job of transforming this organization from a top-down hierarchy to an empowered organization?"** *My first response was, "I'd build teams, train them and turn them loose on challenging assignments, with real power to act."*

So we began a journey that was to be a real education for me and a transforming journey for all of us involved. I worked intensely with that employee team, and we developed five days of training together in the areas of empowerment, leadership, team functioning and responsibility—all the areas that are important in realizing team success.

It was a very important collaboration for me, because they brought the valuable perspectives of employees—how they had been used to operating and the very real needs of the business. I brought some tools, progressive ideas and skill-building approaches that were valuable to the mix. I remember that one of the first concerns expressed was, "We need to have separate classes for different levels of management, because we can't put all levels together in the same room. No one would talk or interact." But we decided that we would put everyone together as a symbolic statement that said, "We're all in this together, and we need to start communicating."

As we began the arduous task of building teams, we experienced a lot of resistance to change. But we also saw many teams begin to take hold of new tools and new ideas and gel as teams and get some exciting progress made. We also observed a lot of teams that were dead in the water and still arguing about trivial things and getting nowhere. So I interviewed some of the most successful and least successful teams to find out what the key differences were. The model you'll see emerged from this research, and it has been an important blueprint for building teams ever since.

---

**Everyone experienced amazing change from being integrally involved in the journey toward transforming work groups into high-performing teams.**

---

In all, I spent about four years working inside that organization. We put 750 people through five days of training, much of it with intact teams. The net effect during that period was that the organization met its aggressive goals through the efforts of hundreds of dedicated people and the success of many teams. The organization was transformed, and by the end of that period, they were truly in a totally different business, with totally different mindsets about who they were and what their jobs were. That division has evolved and is now known as Global Services, which has consistently been one of IBM's highest revenue-generating divisions. Everyone experienced amazing change from being integrally involved in the journey toward transforming work groups into high-performing teams.

I was transformed, too. What I understood theoretically before had changed and evolved dramatically. I saw firsthand what noninvolvement meant to a team's effectiveness. I experienced for myself the importance of understanding the mix of personalities and the dynamics of that mix in a team setting. I saw for myself the devastating effects of what happens when a manager is controlling and won't let go enough to give the team real decision-making responsibility. I understood the reality of a team that is in constant conflict and the impact of people just giving up rather than really working it out.

I had a new respect for people and a new belief in the unlimited power of people working together to accomplish any goal—even ones that seemed out of reach. I became a more passionate advocate, a better coach and a more insightful trainer than I had ever been before because of my experience at IBM.

The model that you see here is a culmination of the research and interviews we did at IBM as well as the answers to the question, "What are the differences between high-performing teams and the low-performing teams that are getting nothing done?" Those are answers that everyone involved with teams needs to understand thoroughly.

In the model, you'll see three levels of team functioning. Actually, there's a fourth level. Down at the bottom of the pyramid is a level we called a "clump." This is where people show up in the same location in the building and know each other's names and are relatively polite—but that's about the extent of the connection! Some of you may recognize this as a characteristic of your own work situation.

**ELEMENTS CRITICAL TO TEAM SUCCESS**

# THREE LEVELS OF TEAM FUNCTIONING

### High Performance Team

Passionate
commitment to a
mission that matters.
A Force to be reckoned with.
Shared Vision, Shared Values.
Strong Sense of Loyalty.
Pride in Identity.
Relationship / People know each member's
strengths and skills.
The glue that holds us together
Shared leadership.
High trust and respect.
Highest levels of involvement and commitment
to tasks and each other.
Extraordinary results--exceeds expectations.

### Team
Shared goals.
Common purpose.
Emerging identity "us".
Tasks - the glue that holds us together - Hands off.
Moderate level of involvement and commitment.

### Group
Individual goals, personal agendas are primary.
Definable membership - "I, Me, Mine."
Sense of group consciousness. - High conflict, territorial.
Convenience holds us together. - Leader driven.
Lower levels of involvement and commitment.

## "CLUMP"

## Characteristics of Groups

The first level of team functioning is the group. This is a collection of individual workers who still have their own separate work goals as their primary agendas. They have an "I, me, mine" focus, which means they are thinking about their own assignments and not about how everything fits together. What you hear from this type of worker is, "I can't stand all the meetings I have to go to! Don't they know I have a real job to do? I wish people would just leave me alone and let me do my work!" It's not surprising that people have an individual focus at work. This is how the workplace has been built, around individuals performing tasks and reporting to their managers, who interact with them on a one-on-one basis. Pay systems are built around this model, and people are reinforced and rewarded on this basis. It is a very strong paradigm to break out of, but it is the first major challenge—transforming from an individual work mindset to a true team mindset.

Another characteristic of groups is that they have definable membership. They know which department or team they are assigned to. There is occasional cooperation and teamwork, but that is different than a true team effort. The work group is characterized by high conflict, because all of these individual agendas are bumping up against one another. There is a lot of territorialism and turf protection, because each person is guarding her own territory and thinking about her own priorities. This is what produces an organization trapped in a "silo mentality." Everyone is thinking only about her own piece of the business but not feeling responsible for the success of the whole.

---

**It is a very strong paradigm to break out of, but it is the first major challenge—transforming from an individual work mindset to a true team mindset.**

---

A group is leader-driven, which means that there is a person in charge who makes everything happen, and others fall in line with his or her directions. At this level, managers or team leaders tend to retain high control and interact with individuals as their main mode of communication. If managers are unwilling to let go of being in control and let their team take ownership, the team will never mature. The manager has to switch from managing each individual's work to creating the environment for team success as well as supporting and coaching the team.

To grow as a team, the leader has to engage the minds and hearts of everyone involved. It is the team's involvement in developing and owning its purpose and goals that produces the initial engagement and creates a feeling of ownership. Once team members have a sense of ownership of the successful achievement of their goal, the group has crossed the line into team territory!

## Characteristics of Teams

The second level is the team level. As you just read, one thing that causes a group of people to become a team is a shared goal and a common purpose. The agenda changes! It now becomes, "We all own responsibility for achieving this goal together." This shared sense of ownership around a unifying goal is critical for teams in order to cross the line between functioning as a group and functioning as a team. It is critical whether the team is an intact departmental team, a project team or a cross-functional team. All teams must first share this sense of responsibility for achieving their goals.

---

**...one thing that causes a group of people to become a team is a shared goal and a common purpose.**

---

---

## Avoid the Deadly "Poof" Syndrome

Many times, organizations rely on what I call the "Poof" syndrome. They know teams are all the rage, so they get out their magic wand, wave it and say "Poof! You all are teams now!" But that is about the extent of the change they make. They don't create environments in which teams can flourish. They don't equip teams with new skills. They don't allocate time to laying a foundation of understanding about what it takes to build a team. They don't train managers in how to manage and interact with a team, instead of managing people one on one. They don't even give teams a map of the teambuilding journey. That's why the Three Levels Map has been so valuable over the years. It serves as a map of the teambuilding journey and gives us some important reference points to use in the team-development process.

## Create a Team Identity

Once the team feels responsibility for a shared goal and a common purpose, it needs to address its own identity. This isn't a factor that I was searching for initially, but it emerged in the research we did. Teams that were making progress had developed a shared language. They had a "we, us, ours" sense instead of an "I, me, mine" sense. I saw this happen when Denver got a new professional baseball team. There were big "Name the Team" contests on the radio, and the search was on for the best team logo. Soon it was announced that the franchise name would be the Rockies. Their colors were purple and black, and they had a logo and a mascot, too. Now the team had an identity. The community rallied around Rockies, and everyone was talking about them. What we learned in the interviews was that team identity is an important part of team development. We began to have work teams name themselves and adopt little mascots or door posters or other symbols of who they were collectively.

## Hand-Offs Are Critical

Did you know that a track relay team can run a mile faster than an individual can? That's why the team is always working on one thing—the hand-offs. They have to be flawless, so they practice and perfect them in order to get better. It is important for teams to perfect the same thing. Each person has to know his own role and know where the hand-offs come in order for the team to execute with excellence. Often, team roles and assignments aren't addressed early and clearly, and it always causes problems, missed assignments, missed expectations and a disillusioned (or even disqualified) team.

## Teams Have Transactional Impact

At the team level, there is a moderate amount of involvement and excitement. People have to balance their individual agendas with the team agenda. For some teams, this is the appropriate level to aspire to. A task force that comes together for six weeks with a very specific assignment would do well to move from an initial clump to a team, and that would be the appropriate level for them. At this level, the connection is all about the work, so the effect on people is a transactional impact. After the work is done, the team members go their separate ways, and usually the connections between the people dissipate, too. The connections are around the work, and when the work is gone, the connection is gone.

## The Fascinating Differences in High-Performing Teams

The highest level of team functioning turned out to be the most interesting. We weren't looking for another level, but it definitely emerged, and we found it very valuable when it came to employees understanding the characteristics of teams that transcend the team level. First of all, the team has a passionate commitment to a mission that matters, which involves a different level of emotion invested. Members develop a shared vision and a shared set of values and experience a shared mindset around what they are doing. Now, instead of an emerging identity, they have a strong pride in identity. Not only do they have this within the team but others around them pick up on it. They become known in much broader circles than just their own. They literally become a force to be reckoned with. They can make things happen. They begin to feel their influence and their collective power, and it feeds the energy and excitement even more. At this level, the team members will literally sacrifice their own personal agendas for the achievement of the team's agenda. You see people pitching in, doing whatever it takes, working extra hours. They are fully invested in achieving the team's mission, and everyone feels the energy.

---

**The most important difference is that at the high-performing level, relationship is the glue that holds everything together.**

---

The most important difference is that at the high-performing level, relationship is the glue that holds everything together. People know each other well enough to trust each other. There is also high respect and open communication. These team members experience conflict, but they have learned how to disagree and be okay. They have learned to trust each other enough to be open with their concerns, to really hash out the issues, and thus they tend to come up with the best possible decisions. Because of this trust and open communication, when they do make decisions, every team member is highly committed to following through. The team is characterized by extraordinary results, and they often exceed expectations.

When I'm working with teams, I will often ask them to look at the map and ask two questions: "Where are we now?" and "Where do we want to go?" Teams that want to be a force to be reckoned with instinctively recognize this level as critical to achieving their shared mission. Teams that have huge challenging assignments need to be at this level. The employee team at IBM that owned the challenge of transforming its organization over a three-year period needed to be a high-performing team—literally a force to be reckoned with!

## High-Performing Teams Are Transformational

High-performing teams are the pinnacle of teamwork, and their functioning is something that is awesome to experience. There are high levels of creativity, because humans access their most creative energy when they feel strongly about something and are emotionally invested in it. People experience the highest levels of employee satisfaction at this level. In fact, when I ask people to share their experiences with high-performing teams, they always speak in superlatives—"fantastic," "amazing," "energizing," "motivating." I ask them, "Would you expend considerable energy to get back to that place with the team you're on now?" They always say, "Absolutely! It was the best work experience of my life! I was never so proud of anything I did! I will never forget it. In fact, I'm still friends with all the people on that team and keep in touch with all of them." That is another of the important benefits of teamwork at this level; it is transformational in nature. People are fundamentally, positively changed as a result of being a part of this experience. If enough teams develop into high-performing teams, organizations are fundamentally changed as a result .

---

**That is another of the important benefits of teamwork at this level; it is transformational in nature. People are fundamentally, positively changed as a result of being a part of this experience.**

---

## Not a Time-Dependent but a Knowledge-Dependent Process

In my teambuilding sessions, people often ask me, "How long does it take to get all this work done?" They're envisioning huge amounts of time invested and think they can't spare time away from their "real work." I tell them that it isn't a time-dependent process but a knowledge-dependent process. The better you know what elements have to come into place, the faster you can take the team forward. I've worked with many teams to help them plan day-long retreats in which we got a huge amount of bonding and relationship-building accomplished; we wrote their charters or their mission statements, and we established our ground rules and had a set of goals to guide the work—all in one good day.

Teams that don't have the time or the budget to set aside one whole day can accomplish the work by allocating time to building the team in addition to allocating time to do their work. For example, I recently worked with a team at a company called StorageTek, a leading data storage company in Louisville, Colorado. The team was charged with successfully managing the product launch window. They were a cross-functional team, whose responsibility and organizational reach was immense! They met weekly to coordinate activities and plan for next steps in preparation for the product launches. The team had been functioning as a group of individual specialists, so their meetings had consisted of reporting to each other what they were doing and listening to everyone else do the same.

In talking with their team leader and team sponsor, I learned that they were frustrated and felt that their group was capable of much more than it was accomplishing. Their first breakthrough was the insight that they weren't a real team; they were a still a group. They decided they should be a team. Really, they needed to be a force to be reckoned with if they were going to strategically manage the product launch window for this company.

The sponsor and the team leader were sure they didn't even have the right people on the team, because the team wasn't empowered to make decisions. Everyone had to go back and get a sign-off from their department on every decision made, which slowed them down immensely. So the leaders went to work on getting the right departments and the right decision makers involved in the team. Then they got sign-offs by everyone who did have decision-making authority for his or her respective team. For two months, they extended their meeting time from one hour to two hours and allocated the first hour to teambuilding activities. During the time we spent together, they recreated their vision and expanded their reason for being, making it much more strategic in scope and stepping up to take responsibility for making key launch-window decisions. The team wrote a new mission together. Their discussions answered a lot of questions and clarified for all team members what they were actually supposed to accomplish. They brainstormed team goals, which resulted in a much broader set of goals than they had claimed before. It was interesting, because they had some very important members out in the field who met with them by conference call, but they were successfully integrated into this process and contributed a great deal.

I helped facilitate a role-negotiation exercise, in which each member made a flip chart of what he understood his role to be. As we reviewed them, we saw that most of the things listed were task-level items. (That wasn't surprising, but it was affirmation that they had not been thinking or acting on the strategic level.) Since the new mission of the team was to make strategic decisions about how and when products would be launched, they all needed to update and expand their role definitions. The discussions expanded and clarified the responsibilities of each key player.

An important part of the role negotiation was brainstorming a list of expectations about their executive sponsor's role. They wrote down everything, refined, discussed and then presented it to her (a vice president of marketing.) She suggested some changes and additions but was very pleased and supportive and became an active part of their success, because she knew exactly what to do to contribute to the team's progress and results.

I can't emphasize enough how important upper-level sponsorship is to the success of teams.

---

**Having a champion who understands, commissions the team, acts as an advocate for it and helps team members secure the resources they need is critical.**

---

**ELEMENTS CRITICAL TO TEAM SUCCESS**

# THE FOUR ESSENTIAL "R'S" OF BUILDING TEAMS

### RESULTS

Meeting management participation.

Shared decision-making accountability.

Climate for creativity.

Recognition.

Process evaluation.

### ROLES

Role clarity.

Role flexibility.

Role expansion.

Sharing the load.

Shared leadership.

### RELATIONSHIPS

Understanding each other / valuing differences.

Open communication / trust appreciation.

Surfacing issues.

Managing conflict positively.

Listening.

### REASONS FOR BEING

Mission / vision / clear purpose.

Shared goals and shared values.

Operating agreements and ground rules.

Identity.

## Team Functioning

*Teams Need to Cover All the Bases*

Once the members have agreed on the type of team they want to become, they have the beginnings of a shared vision. Now they can lay the foundation for their team's development. The second map, The Four Essential R's of teambuilding, helps them visualize the bases that need to be covered. As you can see, the team needs to address its reason for being, which includes visioning and writing a mission statement, developing a set of shared goals, discussing shared values and agreeing on the ground rules.

Second, the team members need to spend some time getting to know things about each other—not just surface facts but things like work style preferences, communication skills, background, experiences, and history. You can't adequately deploy the skills and talents of team members if they don't know anything about each other. It is essential for teams to spend time on exercises that open up communication and build trust. The team needs to clarify each person's role and address how each is going to cross-train team members to enhance coverage and flexibility. (My space in this chapter is limited, so I can't include exercises and resources to help you with this, but please give me a call, because I have wonderful resources and assessments to build relationships and assess the level of trust in teams.)

Finally, team members need to learn new skills, usually in meeting management, conflict resolution, trust building and making decisions using effective processes. This map will help you plan the various activities that need to occur in the early days of team formation.

## It's Important for the Team to Vision Together

You may have heard the famous quote, "Without a vision, the people perish." But often, the manager or the sponsor—the person who formed the team—tells the people very little about why they are a team or what they are supposed to accomplish. The team sponsor needs to share an inspiring vision so the team will have in their minds a compelling reason for existence. Having an inspiring vision helps the team get off to a positive start and gain momentum right away, knowing it is heading in the right direction.

---

**The team sponsor needs to share an inspiring vision so the team will have in their minds a compelling reason for existence.**

---

Set up a time for the team to vision together. This means engaging in out-of-the-box, blue-sky thinking together. Some questions they could address are:

- What could our team contribute that would make a positive difference for our company?
- Of all the things we could accomplish, which would be the most important?
- What would we do if we had no limits (no budget, no time, no personnel limits)?
- Why is it important that we do this one thing really well?
- What could each of us gain by being involved?
- Why am I excited, passionate about being involved?

After you've had this discussion, clarify for the team what a mission statement is. The definition I like best is:

**A statement of who we are and what we are commissioned to achieve—in the present.**

Similarly, a "vision" is defined as:

## A statement of what we have the potential to become.

I like to see teams write a mission statement that is visionary but contained in one memorable statement.

## Mission Statements Have to Contain an Element of Passion

When most teams write a mission statement, they end up with dull, boring, left-brained business definitions that are too long, uninspiring, and never get used.

Your team's job is to write a brief, memorable statement that captures the essence of why it exists. It should have an element of emotion and passion in it. It should be easy to remember and repeat. It needs to identify the team's unique value-added contribution. "Quality is Job One" is a short, memorable statement, but it has nothing in it that couldn't apply to 10,000 companies.

The most important thing to remember about a mission statement is this:

**The process of *creating* the mission statement is much more important than the mission statement itself. The shared experience of creating it brings clarity, instills a feeling of ownership, causes people to engage and connects with the motivation and the passion they feel for what they're about to undertake.**

## How to Write a Mission Statement in Thirty Minutes or Less!

Teams need a good, efficient process for writing a mission statement that involves everyone's thinking. Once members understand each other's thinking about the vision and what a mission statement is, get them started this way:

**Step One:** Give out three sticky notes and a Sharpie marker to each participant.

Ask team members to write one short phrase on each of their three sticky notes. Each phrase should be something that they feel is central to their mission. "If we could only say three things about what we're here to do, they would be…" Ask them to include words of passion as well as talk about what is exciting and the value added to it, not just a definition of it.

**Step Two:** Ask everyone on the team to share what they wrote.

Put the stickies up on a board. Have the team sort them into groups by theme. There should be several strong areas of agreement in your group. Get agreement about what these areas are and identify the themes by name.

**Step Three:** Have each team member write one statement that combines these themes. Encourage them to use the phrases they like best.

**Step Four:** Read the statements to the team. The team should listen and choose one that captures best (most succinctly, most clearly, most passionately) what you want to identify as your team mission. (I find that it's usually the one that makes everyone say "Ooh!" Try to assess the team's strongest response and go with that.)

**Step Five:** Finish the process by shuffling words in and out of the "base phrase" until everyone is satisfied. Give yourself a time limit and agree not to wordsmith it forever.

If you need to do this in two meetings rather than one, do Steps One and Two to identify the theme areas. Give everyone the homework assignment of developing his or her one statement and e-mailing it to you. Compile everyone's statements and complete steps Three, Four and Five at your next meeting.

The goal is to get everyone engaged, get creativity flowing, and get everyone focused on the team's mission without belaboring it to the point where people get disgusted with the process and lose interest.

## How to Get the Team to Stop Squabbling About Who's Doing What—A Fascinating Approach to Roles

I gave you a brief snapshot of how we negotiated roles in the story about the product launch team. That was an activity that I highly recommend and I always facilitate, when possible. However, another helpful approach to getting teams to talk about roles is to use an assessment called a *Team Dimensions Profile*. (It is published by InScape Publishing, and you can get it through me or any InScape representative.)

## Here are some of the pitfalls that teams fall into:

One type of team goes with the first solution presented and runs with it, regardless of the quality or feasibility of the concept. Team members don't want to rock the boat by disagreeing or questioning anyone's ideas.

Another type of team has two or three members who dominate the group. They are strong communicators and aren't afraid to shoot holes in everyone else's ideas.

Another type of team has too many idea people, so all they do is generate ideas and argue about which one is the best. But they don't seem to agree on how to proceed toward the goal.

## Insights About Roles From the Team Dimensions Profile

The Team Dimensions Profile is a self-scored assessment that can help team members understand their preferred styles and their best contributions to the team's process. The assessment identifies five distinct roles played by members of the team.

The first role is **Creator**. This is the person who loves to come up with ideas and solutions. She often gives birth to many of the breakthroughs and innovative changes. Often, she sees the big picture and thinks outside the box as she operates.

The second role is the **Advancer**. He instinctively recognizes a good idea or a breakthrough concept and begins to think immediately about how to take it forward. His focus is on selling the idea and advancing it through levels of decision makers, in the marketplace or with the rest of the team. Once he gets on board with an idea, he is a very strong advocate of it.

The third role is the **Refiner**. Her preferred role is analyzing ideas to detect potential problems and challenge them. Her contributions help the team refine and get the bugs out of what they already have. It's not always a popular role, but it's an important one to recognize and appreciate in overall team success. A team heavy on Refiners can tear every idea to shreds and not advance quickly enough toward implementation of the plan. Or they may forget to sell the idea before they perfect the plan.

The fourth role is **Executor**. This person is strong in planning, thinking at the detail level, implementing and carrying through with plans. He doesn't necessarily want to brainstorm ideas all day long. He just wants to select the best idea, get a great plan with clear assignments and go forward toward the goal.

The fifth role is the **Facilitator**. Her role is to serve as a facilitator to keep the process moving forward, serve as a communicator between different types of contributors and help "grease the skids" as these different styles come into conflict.

You can imagine how important it is to have teams that are balanced and have all the roles represented. Team members need to be aware of their natural tendencies and be able to deploy people at the right times in the right assignments. The assessment gives the team knowledge and respect for each other's most natural roles and helps them develop a common language to deal with differences in approach.

---

**Team members need to be aware of their natural tendencies, and be able to deploy people at the right time in the right assignments. This is what "perfecting the hand-offs" is all about.**

---

## The Z-Process of Innovation

A technique that can be used in conjunction with these roles is the Z-process of Innovation. If you imagine the letter Z, the Creators start at the top left of the Z. They come up with amazing ideas and a conceptual plan and hand these off to the Advancers at the top right of the Z, who figure out how to get the idea sold. Once they have support, they pass it—imagine it sliding down the middle of the Z—to the Refiners at the bottom left of the Z, who figure out the detail of the plan and what is missing in the approach. They find the needles in the haystack and may pass the plan back to the Advancers and Creators for more work. (Facilitators can help with this back-and-forth communication, up and down the angle of the Z!) When the plan finally passes muster with the Refiners, it goes forward to the Executors at the bottom right of the Z, who like the role of taking the necessary steps to make things happen. Facilitators keep the process moving forward. Each has a very important but very different strength and a different natural contribution. It doesn't mean that everyone doesn't contribute to every phase of the team process, but it does mean that different team members will provide the impetus for forward movement at different times. Knowing this information can help teams build trust, open up communication and make progress toward their goals.

## The Importance of Leadership

We can't fail to mention how important the leader is to team success! I can't tell you the number of times I have seen teams fail because they had no leadership or the wrong person was in charge of the team. Many mistakenly think that leaders fail because they are lazy or uncommitted or don't care about the team's success or don't know anything about how to motivate people.

Actually, many failures happen when the leader is too ambitious and cares too much about the team's success. These leaders are totally committed and want the team to succeed in the worst way. Because of all these factors, they very often fall into the trap of being an over-responsible leader. They take on 200 percent of the responsibility for making the team succeed. They do almost everything themselves and don't let go enough to really allow the team to have ownership and feel shared responsibility for the team's success.

## Heroic Leaders Create Passive Followers

---

**The irony is that heroic leaders, as much as they want to succeed, will inevitably fail, because their approach creates passive or under-responsible followers.**

---

The irony is that heroic leaders, as much as they want to succeed, will inevitably fail, because their approach creates passive or under-responsible followers. A leader who communicates, either overtly or with innuendoes ("I'm in charge, and you're not!") will inevitably produce people around him who are under-responsible. It is the only possible response people can make—even really talented people who want to make great contributions. The unspoken deal that goes into place is that when the leader takes charge, the others acquiesce, thinking, "Okay, hotshot. Let's see you make this happen by yourself." People who surround heroic leaders develop learned helplessness. They learn that if they try something and the leader doesn't want it that way, the leader will change it or fix it to be the way he/she wants. So they give up trying. They learn that if they don't follow through with an assigned task, the leader will step in and do it. If they sit there helpless long enough, the leader will get frustrated and give up or ask someone else. Negative feelings develop as the leader thinks no one is capable or responsible or cares enough to lift a finger! Team members get resentful of the leader who acts like he knows everything, controls everything and decides about everything.

> Successful team leaders are the leaders who send the
> message, "We're all in this together. It's going to take
> all of us contributing our special skills and talents to
> achieve this goal." These leaders allow people to really
> make decisions, really own responsibility and be ac-
> countable for their actions. They have freedom to
> operate within agreed-upon parameters, and they have
> clear goals and well-defined roles, so the leader can
> trust them, turn them loose and let them operate.

Great team leaders are those who have learned how to engage people in the processes we've discussed: laying the
foundation by visioning together, determining their mission,
setting their goals, creating their action plan and making decisions that demonstrate true ownership and responsibility.
(These concepts are from the book *The Responsibility Virus* by
Roger Martin.)

### A True Team Success Story

One of my best client experiences was with First Data Corporation, a leading Fortune 500 Financial Services company. I
had an opportunity to work within their finance/CFO organization. I encountered them when they had just experienced a
merger. Western Union, a company with a hundred years of
tradition and well developed systems for everything, merged
with First Data Corporation, a younger, more maverick type of
organization. My first assignment was to facilitate teambuilding to help them merge two finance-related teams into one
cohesive team. As a result of that introduction, I gained a thorough understanding of their growth challenges.

The leader of the finance division at that time was Kim
Patmore, whom I came to know well. I knew her to be one of
the best, most complete executives I have ever encountered.
She had an exciting vision for the CFO organization at that
time. She wanted them to be the most progressive organization
in the First Data enterprise. She wanted every employee to

think of herself as a business partner with the organizational group she supported. Kim wanted to train and develop leaders in her division who could move into key leadership positions and have an impact all over the organization. She wanted the CFO organization to be leading-edge and launch innovative programs that were so good for people and for business that they were adopted throughout the company.

One day, when we were on a trip together, she received the results of an employee survey. Many of the categories were scored much lower than she liked, and she was discouraged. As we talked, she said, "I just don't know what else I can do to get a turnaround in these areas. We've been working so hard, and it barely shows that we've made any progress. I am just tired of trying to make all these people happy."

The same thought I had shared with the IBM team—"I'd put together teams, give them real power to act and make them responsible for finding solutions to these problems"—came to my mind. I shared my first thought: "You and your management team can't possibly be responsible for making this a better organization all by yourself!" She had been thinking exactly the same thoughts, so she commissioned several teams to address the problem areas. She asked me if I would work with the teams—equip, train and coach them—and work within her organization to help make the teams as successful as possible.

As our leader, she totally empowered us, putting real money in team budgets and authorizing us to make decisions, take action and find solutions. She legitimized the time that employees could devote to team projects. She created rewards and fun ways to recognize and encourage teams. In doing this, she did her strategic job as an organizational leader. She created an environment in which the teams could be successful, and she committed to equipping teams with the skills they needed to succeed. She shared her vision and told us, "If we're going to make this organization a great place to work, it's going to take all of us working together to make that happen." Then she really let go and let us all spread our wings! Now that's great leadership, and that's empowerment in action—not just words and lip service.

There was a lot of excitement and energy flowing! The teams went to work and came up with some really great ideas. The team that was responsible for addressing how to retain people and facilitate career growth came up with the idea of launching a mentor program. They were in total agreement that this initiative would make the most impact on career growth and retention. They began researching, structuring their program, figuring out how to make good matches between senior-level people and the goals of staff-level people. They recruited many impressive senior-level people to be mentors. One of the committees established its match criteria and personally involved itself in discussing each one until the members were sure they had the best possible match. In addition to working behind the scenes with ideas and coaching, I was asked to develop and present the mentor training, which was a great privilege for me! It meant I got to be a "player" and a part of the rollout of the new program, too! This was exciting, because I was feeling a lot of ownership at that point, as were all the other team members. The teams successfully promoted the program and planned an elaborate kickoff. In the first rollout, we had ninety people involved in matches, and excitement was high.

---

**Now, 30,000 people have the opportunity to be involved in a mentor relationship because of the work and commitment of that one great employee team that had the vision and the ownership to make it a reality**

---

The program turned out to be so successful that other locations wanted to have a mentor program, so the original employee team helped teams in other locations get set up for successful launches, too. The mentor program's popularity snowballed, and soon the entire CFO organization was involved. It continued to be so highly evaluated that it was finally agreed upon that the whole organization needed to have access to a mentor program, so it was rolled out company-wide. Now, 30,000 people have the opportunity to be involved in a mentor relationship because of the work and commitment of that one great employee team that had the vision and the ownership to make it a reality. It was truly a great team success story and one that will always bc one of my career highlights.

## Where Do We Go From Here?

The impact of culture-changing initiatives like this can't be underestimated. It had far-reaching, organization-wide impact, and it sent important messages about the importance of employees, the importance of their development, the belief in their ability to contribute and make a difference, and the fundamental values of the organization. I knew it was a culture-changing initiative when I heard employees talking about it as one of the reasons they liked working for First Data Corporation.

I am convinced that my most important work in the next ten years will be helping companies to conceptualize, plan and build high-performing teams that will implement similar initiatives to transform their organizations into *high-involvement, high-responsibility cultures.* There is much work to be done in helping high-control managers learn how to stop being heroic leaders and learn how to inspire and mobilize the "want-to" motivation that is so important to high achievement! There is much work to be done in changing the paradigm from individuals doing their best to exceeding all limits by achieving true team synergy!

All companies are struggling right now with how to get employees to be accountable and how to achieve their *full engagement.* We must be sophisticated and dedicated to finding the right way to achieve this important end. Some companies are approaching the task with higher-demand and higher-control initiatives, such as creating stringent performance standards and measures to get people to raise the bar and achieve higher levels of performance. My belief is that organizations need to ultimately be moving toward building more freedom and responsibility, as well as accountability into the environments they create.

The way that people enter into contributing at their highest level is to have a strong want-to motivation rather than a strong have-to motivation. We don't get people's discretionary efforts until their hearts are engaged! We will not achieve high-performance environments by creating more measures, but we will achieve high performance as we understand and trust that people want to give their best. It is executive leadership's most important role to create the environment in which people want to give you everything they've got. What employees need is high involvement so they have a true sense of ownership and pride, clearly defined parameters to give them direction and security, real responsibility and authority that demonstrates their leader's trust and genuine freedom to create, operate and fully spread their wings and fly.

---

**We don't get people's discretionary efforts until their hearts are engaged!**

---

As we commit to creating the environment for every employee's success and gain the knowledge needed to build high-performance teams, we will surely achieve it all—true freedom, true ownership, high responsibility and high accountability. We will achieve the truly extraordinary results that happen only in high-performance organizations.

## About The Author

### Jan Baller

Jan Baller is the President of **POTENTIAL PLUS+.** Over the last twenty years, she has become a specialist in organizational, team, and personal transformation. She assists executive teams in creating a RESPONSIBILITY CULTURE—one built on trust, not high control, and one that achieves high performance business results. She serves as a coach in building high-performing teams, trains/coaches managers to transform themselves into empowering, inspiring leaders, and trains/coaches individuals to grow into highly responsible, confident, outstanding contributors. Regardless of the assignment, her goal is always the same—*transforming potential into power.*

*Her amazing programs help companies create accountability and achieve the results they have targeted. Whether it's a new approach to Performance Management, a new approach to building high-performance teams, or a new approach to engaging employees through excellent leadership, she makes her presence felt, and her efforts make a difference!*

She brings vision, passion, energy, hope, and heart to transform people's thinking and revolutionize their approaches to achieving superior results. Clients of Jan's include: First Data Corporation, Western Union, J.D. Edwards, StorageTek, Big O Tires, Wells Fargo, I.B.M., U.S. Department of Interior, Sears Roebuck and company, Wal-Mart, Lennox Furnace, Maytag, The Principal Financial Group, Hewlett-Packard, Gates Rubber Company, US West, and many more.

Jan Baller
7790 S. Buchanan Way
Aurora, CO 80016
Office: 303.368.9541
Cell: 303.994.0878
Fax: 303.368.0476
Email: janballer@comcast.net
Web: www.potentialplus.org

# Chapter Six

## Beyond Blindfolds:
## Teambuilding That Works

### Dr. Jacalyn Sherriton and James L. Stern

## What Does Teambuilding Really Mean?

### *How People View Teambuilding Today*

After spending twenty-six years building high-performance teams for diversified industries, our management-consulting firm has noted that the concept of teambuilding means different things to different organizations, leaders and team members. These perceptions are often based on past experiences, good and bad, as well as what the words associated with those experiences have come to represent.

What comes to your mind first when someone says, "Let's have a teambuilding event"? Do you think of climbing mountains, swinging from ropes or singing "Kumbaya"? Perhaps fun-filled games, happy hour or a golf outing come to mind. Then there is the thought of being blindfolded, having to trust your team to catch you when you fall.

How do these teambuilding exercises make you feel? Are you excited about the lightheartedness of such experiences? Do they bring to mind a memorable round of golf or a good laugh? Do you dread the possibility of being embarrassed by a physical activity due to your lack of agility? Do you fear having to trust a team member in a game when you have never trusted that person in real life? Are you annoyed at having to spend time on something frivolous when you have more important things to do? These reactions are all natural, given what teambuilding experiences have often represented in the past.

Teambuilding activities have become common in the workplace. Countless teambuilding events are often squeezed into short time frames, as opening ice breakers or mini-events. Unrealistically, some of these fun, short-duration activities are expected to be a cure-all or panacea for deeply-rooted team problems. Others are thought of as just "the right thing to do" when the team is together. Many activities are actually intended to avoid team issues and glaze over unspoken problems.

Events positioned this way often do not make a dent in the team's performance or enhance its ability to perform, and team members' greatest concerns are typically not revealed or addressed. Immediately following such an event, there is an afterglow of fun (assuming the team had fun in the first place), but months down the road, team members rarely remember the specifics. So it's back to business, with the team still tackling or avoiding the same issues they always had. It's no wonder that most people are cynical about teambuilding.

### Teambuilding as a Serious Process

Our firm takes teambuilding events, their objectives, focus and expected outcomes very seriously. Our work involves assisting all types of teams in becoming high performing. This includes helping project teams, executive teams, department teams or interdivisional teams as well as more broadly organizational teams meet their objectives. We build teams proactively, at their initiation phase, to help them get started, as well as reactively, when a team is in trouble midstream.

Our proactive approach lays important groundwork, anticipates potential problems and addresses them before they become obstacles. Similarly, it facilitates agreements on how to operate so future problems are prevented.

Our problem-centered approach focuses on identifying and addressing the critical issues or obstacles that can impact a team. It ensures that resolutions, decisions and action plans are developed.

Regardless of the impetus for building a team, our methodology is consistent. It has proven to be a formula for success, yielding great results and a track record as a serious, substantive approach.

### *A Formula For Success*

## TEAMBUILDING FORMULA FOR SUCCESS
## <u>KEY INGREDIENTS</u>

The key ingredients in our formula work together to produce very clear, measurable outcomes (both quantitative and qualitative) that are linked to the actual work the team is doing. Even when lighter, fun simulations are used to achieve a point, they are always correlated to the team's current situation and a relevant team outcome is assured.

First, it is imperative to have clear objectives for a teambuilding effort. Knowing what is precipitating the event as well as the expected outcomes is an important first step.

Our approach is data driven. Using interviews and a Team Effectiveness Survey, we can efficiently determine a team's strengths and issues. The key issues are identified and used to create a tailored agenda that addresses them in a constructive manner. The data are then shared to develop an understanding of how the agenda was formulated, and activities are structured to help the team confront and resolve those issues. Resolutions, agreements and action plans are developed, and decisions are made to fix current problems and prevent future ones.

Accountability for follow-through is an inherent part of the process. Each team member/leader understands who is responsible for what time frames and follow-up actions. Informal follow-ups are established within the team, and one formal follow-up is scheduled with us at an agreed-upon time. Their purpose is to evaluate successes as well as identify new issues and resolve them.

Since evaluating progress is an inherent part of the follow-up, measurable outcomes are defined both at the initial objective setting as well as during the teambuilding session, and agreed-upon tracking mechanisms are put in place.

As you might guess, when a team reflects on its teambuilding experience with us, it is viewed as a serious process. They know that it is far from being a "blindfolded" event. As a matter of fact, they usually say that constructively confronting their issues is an "eye-opening" experience. Most agree that trust is built through airing and resolving issues that had been gnawing at the team for a long time. All fully understand that it would be impossible to accomplish such results in a one-hour time frame and certainly not just through a fun outing designed to mask or assuage the core issues.

## Making the Case for Teambuilding

### *Teams Are Here to Stay*

Teams are an inherent part of the taxonomy of today's organizations. Formalized teams such as project teams, management teams, departmental teams and interdivisional teams are among the more familiar types. A more informal, and less familiar, use of the word "team" might be found in the context of the organization team.

The need to maximize efficiency and the use of resources has led to the need for new organizational structures. Hierarchies have hindered individual expertise from being tapped outside of one's own department. In turn, organizational structures have been formed to facilitate the use of teams by fluidly moving people across teams and the organization to capitalize on their expertise. These are usually referred to as matrixed team structures.

The global nature of business and organizations has made operating in worldwide teams commonplace. The complex environment of specialists versus generalists has created a critical need for teamwork in order to accomplish work, which requires greater collaboration, communication and coordination amongst specialists.

No matter the type or the reasons for being on them, teams have become the modus operandi for accomplishing work. Everyone has experienced some type of team. "It's going to take teamwork" has become the catchall phrase for rallying together to achieve objectives. It might be broadly used for all organization members to rally support for a change or more narrowly as it applies to a specific team. A crucial competency in today's organizational environment is the ability to ensure high-performance teamwork and smoothly functioning teams.

## Teamwork Does Not Occur Naturally

So if teams and teamwork are a normal part of organizational life, deeply ingrained in its fabric, why is there a need for teambuilding? Why don't all teams operate smoothly given that they are so prevalent? Why isn't teamwork a fully embraced, natural way of operating? Here are a few insights into that subject:

First, teamwork does *not* occur naturally, contrary to popular belief and the expectation that it should after so many years. It actually is antithetical to what is natural in American culture.

For instance, take the the definition of teamwork found in Webster's Dictionary: "work done by a number of associates, all subordinating personal prominence for the good of the whole." What words jump out and grab you in the gut? One sure emotional trigger is the phrase "subordinating personal prominence," with a probable emphasis placed on the word "subordinating."

The word usually conjures up a negative connotation of being subservient. Yet it actually denotes operating at a higher level of understanding and behaving accordingly in the best interests of the team. A high-performing team member manifests this behaviorally in a number of ways, such as listening instead of talking, compromising in strategy or decision making, encouraging others' participation instead of dominating, suppressing personal goals to help the team, doing something unpleasant for the sake of the team, asking for and sharing information, sharing in successes instead of taking all the credit and sharing in failure instead of saying "I told you so." But it sounds a lot simpler to actualize than it is.

The behavioral picture described above exposes the difficulties of truly subordinating personal prominence. These are not natural behaviors for many people striving to succeed. Everything that we learn at a young age is contradictory to that concept. We are encouraged to be individualists, independent and self-sufficient. We are taught to compete for that right! We are certainly not taught to put ourselves second to others.

Our schooling or training, which tends to be highly specialized, places us in very separate, independent fields—neither connected to or knowledgeable of the other. Each specialty is clear and proud of its own contribution, and few specialists are willing to take a back seat to the others, each believing his area of expertise to be the correct one. No wonder it's so difficult to compromise on team decisions!

How many times have you encountered brilliant technical people (or perhaps you are one) on a team, who did not feel the need to interact with the rest of the team? Or they found meetings to be a waste of time or believed that no decision other than their own was the correct one? This occurs more frequently than we might prefer.

In organizations, we operate in silos, not fully understanding much about or coordinating with the other departments to accomplish work. Typically, we throw the work over the wall to another silo, washing our hands of it once its gone. Certainly, there is no feeling of ownership of or concern about what happens thereafter. If something goes wrong, it certainly isn't "our fault". What happened to teamwork?

Most people strive to be good performers, to be stars and to stand out rather than strive to blend in or be unnoticed team players. Motivations for striving to be the star vary from having a sense of pride and accomplishment to wanting recognition and reward to securing a job in a tough market.

Historically, organizations have rewarded individualists and star performers in spite of their inability to "play nice" as team members. All too often, we've seen highly skilled people who were unwilling or unable to work well with others, caused lots of conflict and were never held accountable for it. On the contrary, they were often rewarded for their skilled performance despite their teamwork issues. That type of behavior, in essence, is perpetuated, and the message becomes clear and consistent that subordinating one's own prominence is not expected.

## *Myths Perpetuate Ineffective Teams*

After working with hundreds of teams over the years, we've tracked a number of myths about teamwork that illustrate why serious teambuilding is not utilized more frequently.

The first, as we just addressed, is that teamwork occurs naturally. Suffice it to say that more people can attest to being on malfunctioning teams than on magical ones. That truth will likely continue.

The second myth is that time will cure all. We've all heard the storming and norming theory of teams. Part of this is true; it does take time for teams to gel. However, there are many teams that have been dysfunctional for years and will never gel unless there is an intervention of some sort.

Another common myth is that intelligent professionals can make it work. Actually, the smarter and more educated team members are, the more difficult it is for them to work as a team. Having worked with many postdoctorate scientists and engineers, we see their ongoing struggles to be team players versus individual contributors.

Yet another myth is that personality conflicts are the primary inhibitor of high-performing teams. "If only Jane and Joe were not on the team, we would get so much done!" Don't get us wrong; we believe that conflicts clearly weigh teams down and divert everyone's energy away from focusing on objectives. However, it is not about hoping that the team members embroiled in the conflict will be removed from the team. It is really about knowing how to bring conflicts to the surface and resolve them, regardless of the personalities involved.

The myth that fun retreats ensure a high performing team upon their return to work is the most common misperception about teamwork as we discussed earlier.

One can see that if you believe in any of these myths, it potentially could perpetuate ineffective teamwork. Teambuilding would not be a viable strategy; it would be seen as a waste of time since high performance would eventually develop naturally!

The purpose here is to highlight and, in turn, dispel these myths about teamwork, since they hinder a full appreciation of the complexity of teamwork and the skills required to be a high-performing team. A serious teambuilding approach can provide many of the critical skills that are imperative for optimal teamwork.

### Frustrations of Malfunctioning Teams

To understand why a serious teambuilding process is a necessity rather than just a nicety, all you have to do is experience the frustrations of being on a malfunctioning team. Talk about wasted time: time spent in unproductive meetings, going around in circles on recurring issues, arguing with or avoiding certain people and countless post-meeting "feeding frenzies" where you air your frustrations with colleagues.

We could write another book just about the frustrations of team members and leaders. However, we'll share just a few to make the point. Some will probably sound familiar, but they do vary from team to team.

Team members often complain about unclear or duplicative roles on the team. Others say their skills and expertise haven't been fully utilized or that no one solicits their input in decision making. Some say they never get the information they need, while others complain about too many meetings. Then there are ego and turf battles creating conflicts and extra stress among team members. Of course, you will often hear complaints about a leader's skills or lack thereof.

Team leaders feel many of the same frustrations as well as ones that are unique to their role. Their upsets include team members' lack of buy-in on the goals, follow-through on commitments and meeting deadlines. Then there is the prospect of dealing with the overworked few (which often include the team leader) and those that have checked out of the team process. Dealing with unresolved conflicts, finger pointing and whining can be overwhelming. The leader must also be the mediator between the team and the organization, handling mixed allegiances between the two sides and dealing with issues related to lack of support or resources.

These frustrations are only a sample of the myriad issues impacting a team's performance. Unless they are discovered, constructively confronted and resolved, they will continue to undermine performance. A serious teambuilding process provides a forum for identifying and addressing core issues as well as learning important skills for surviving and thriving as a team. Our approach ensures that.

## Our Approach

### *The Model*

The past twenty-six years have provided us with vast experience; we've had the opportunity to research and observe teams that have been supremely successful as well as those that have wallowed in failure. This research opportunity led to our formulating a High-Performance Team Model that we've used with great success. (We believe in the use of models as tools to ensure success in all of our interventions.)

The High-Performance Team Model provides a road map and catalyst that clearly articulates a path forward. It becomes a point of reference or framework that the team can rely on to provide focus and point to success. The model can be used as a goal for any team; it becomes the core methodology for our teambuilding intervention and acts as an agenda to be followed and tracked. Teams are also encouraged to use the model as a diagnostic tool to assess progress or identify areas where the team may be experiencing problems.

FIGURE 1

**HIGH PERFORMANCE TEAM MODEL**

Goals and Objectives

Roles / Utilization of Resources

Controls and Procedures (Norms)

Problem Solving / Decision Making

Trust / Conflict Resolution

Communication

Experimentation / Creativity

Leadership

Evaluation

© Corporate Management Developers, Inc. 1984

Figure 1 represents the High-Performance Team Model. A short description of each component and how that component may be played out during the teambuilding event is described below.

**Goals/Objectives**

Sometimes a team's goals are clear but not agreed upon. Other times they may be agreed upon but unclear or interpreted differently. However, high-performing teams have goals that are both clear and agreed upon.

In teambuilding, existing team goals may be validated and/or new ones developed to help ensure a common team focus. A philosophy might need to be developed, and a revised mission statement and/or vision statement might be formulated if necessary. Additional goals/objectives relating to teamwork may be developed as well.

## Roles/Utilization of Resources

In high-performing teams, each member, including the leader, has a clear, unambiguous role. Each member's talent and expertise are recognized and fully utilized. Time and budget are used effectively.

In teambuilding, specific group and individual roles may be explored and clarified. The concept of effectively capitalizing on all available resources to address team issues may be examined.

## Controls/Procedures

High-performing teams have norms (rules) for behavior within the team environment that are agreed to and followed.

In teambuilding, the positive and negative impact that these norms have on team members and the work environment may be discussed. Action plans for developing improved norms and minimizing counterproductive norms could be negotiated if necessary. Guidance for specific procedures or constraints can be developed. Any spending or budget-related guidelines or time-accounting procedures could be generated.

## Problem Solving/Decision Making

High-performing teams are adept at making good decisions that are supported and implemented. They are able to utilize a variety of tools to solve problems effectively and efficiently.

In teambuilding, problem-solving and decision-making processes might be examined. A variety of alternative techniques can be presented and applied in addressing current team issues and problems. Guidelines for decision-making authority for teams at various levels may be developed and decision-making mechanisms agreed upon.

## Trust/Conflict Resolution

High-performing teams exhibit and rely on trust among members. They understand how conflict drains a team and have the skills and the willingness to address and resolve any conflicts.

In teambuilding, the concept of and need for trust may be explored. Particular skills and techniques for developing trust and resolving conflict could be presented and practiced. Any existing team conflict would be addressed through the application of specific conflict-resolution models.

## Communication

High-performing teams practice three aspects of team communications: (1) good interpersonal communication within and outside the team, (2) good group dynamics as a team function and (3) information sharing.
In teambuilding, these may be discussed to help ensure optimal team results, and agreements could be made to ensure effective communication for the team's specific circumstances. Communication procedures might be identified. Reporting requirements of the team to their customers/clients/managers may be developed. Sharing of information across teams and team members could be emphasized and methods to do so developed.

## Experimentation/Creativity

High-performing teams require the use of explicit mechanisms to focus the creative energy of team members and must be willing to spend the time to realize that benefit.

In teambuilding, techniques can be provided where needed to bring innovative solutions to actual team issues.

## Leadership

High-performing teams exercise the concept of shared leadership and power. This is a broader definition than traditional leadership. It implies that all team members feel equally responsible for the success of the team and take action accordingly.

In teambuilding, specific leadership roles may be pinpointed as shared roles to enhance team performance. Various aspects of power may be explored to provide the catalyst for teams to assume accountability for their own power. Team leadership criteria and requirements might be agreed to or leadership roles assigned.

## Evaluation

Teams typically evaluate results. High-performing teams have an additional focus for evaluating the team process.

In teambuilding, the importance of the "how" in team performance is stressed. Actual team dynamics would be typically observed and feedback used to develop action plans for improvement. Standards for success could be developed as a benchmark to assess the progress and success of the team.

## *The Methodology*

Our methodology begins with a very efficient but in-depth assessment of the current status of the team. We feel this up-front data gathering is essential for the success of building the team. We use a structured interview guide developed specifically for each client team. Our interviews are designed to reveal the positive attributes of the team and its environment as strengths upon which to build. The interview guide also ensures that we identify the issues, concerns and/or obstacles the team is experiencing. We typically interview each team member when working with small teams but use a "focused group" data-gathering technique for larger teams.

In addition to the interviews, we administer to all team members a short Team Effectiveness Survey that corresponds to the High-Performance Team Model. This survey provides a quantitative assessment of team performance along with the qualitative interview data to more accurately analyze current team behavior/performance. The result of the survey becomes a baseline for follow-up comparison after the teambuilding phase.

Over the years, we've accumulated a normative database comprised of survey results from teams we've assessed and worked with over the most current three-year period. The database is refreshed frequently as new team data are added.

## FIGURE 2

### Corporate Management Developers, inc.
### Team Effectiveness Survey
### Normative Means Time I – Time II Comparison

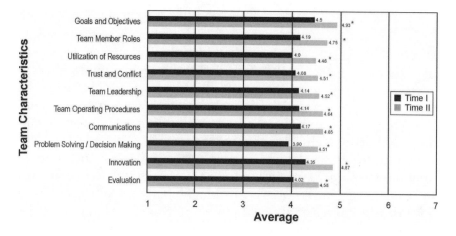

Data set consists of 35 organizations that have responded to both the Time I and Time II Surveys

Time I  N=906
Time II  N=786

** All Time II results are statistically more positive than Time I

Figure 2 represents the normative database with pre/post teambuilding comparisons. Note that every variable shows a statistically significant improvement between the pre- and post-teambuilding periods—a quantifiable testimony that the High-Performance Team Model and our teambuilding methodology work and are effective.

All of these data are analyzed using the High-Performance Team Model as a structure to synopsize patterns and trends that surface. When plugged into the model, these patterns and trends are used to determine the agenda and subsequent exercises used during the teambuilding activity.

## *The Event*

The major event, of course, is the teambuilding retreat. Through a facilitated, efficient process, the retreat addresses whatever needs have surfaced in the assessment/data-gathering phase. The retreat tends to be an intense exchange of ideas, thoughts, concepts and feelings among participants. Conflicts may arise that have to be dealt with and resolved, and decisions are made that dictate the future course of the team and the careers of its members. This is not the typical retreat where participants play golf and free time is built in for a lot of social activities. It is an intense work session, often going into the late hours of the evening. The retreat provides a forum where it's okay to challenge direction and offer differing perspectives. It also provides the structure necessary to deal with issues effectively and constructively.

The retreat is normally conducted over two or three days. The time is dictated by the results of the data analysis.

Following some general introductory activities (such as introductions, an icebreaker, establishing norms and sharing the event's goals and agenda), the retreat begins in earnest with a briefing to the participants, in which the results of the assessment/data-gathering are presented and discussed. This ensures that everyone agrees with the data and that the agenda and topics of the retreat are tied directly to the real issues and concerns of the team.

Each component of the model—used overall as the foundation for developing high-performance teams—is explored during the retreat through a variety of exercises tailored to address specific issues gleaned through the assessment/data-gathering process. These issues may relate to the team's inter-workings, or they may be specific issues the team needs to address in its relationship to the rest of the organization or its project. Skills necessary to ensure successful team functioning are practiced as issues are resolved. Each component results in an agreement, decision or action plan. Team members are expected to live up to agreements made to ensure their continued high performance.

## *The Follow-Up*

Approximately three to four months following the team-building retreat, we recommend a one-day follow-up session. In preparation for the follow-up, we will administer the Team Effectiveness Survey a second time and compare results to those gathered during the initial assessment/data-gathering. We will also conduct abbreviated interviews with a sample of team members. The purpose and goals for the follow-up session are:

- To analyze progress on teamwork
- To assess action plans and commitments made during the teambuilding session
- To identify and celebrate successes
- To identify team areas needing improvement or problems encountered in implementing changes
- To develop strategies to overcome obstacles
- To define current issues and new challenges that need to be addressed for improved teamwork and to create an appropriate action plan

This follow-up process serves not only to accomplish the above goals but to hold the team accountable for results.

## Anecdotal Uses of Our Model

In our work over the years, we've encountered (it seems) almost every issue, problem or dysfunction that a team could encounter. These issues have spanned all of the components of the High-Performance Team Model. Following are some examples of what we've run across and how we approached them during teambuilding retreats.

## *The Recommendation Team*

Following the merger of two petro-chemical companies, we were asked to work with a joint team that had been chartered to make a recommendation to senior management about which of two competing technologies should be employed to ensure the safe operation of refineries. Obviously, one technology had been developed by one heritage company and the other technology by the other company. Over time, the team found itself in severe conflict about selecting one technology over the other. In fact, the conflict had superseded the decision-making process, and the team was quickly approaching its deadline to submit a recommendation.

We were able to assist the team by concentrating on three components of the model. First, under the aegis of the Goals component, we had the team revisit its primary goal to clarify it. Then we helped the team understand and deal with the dynamics of the culture clash that had been in play since the merger. (This is one of our specific areas of expertise.)

Second, when addressing the Trust and Conflict Resolution component of the model, we employed a conflict-resolution model we devised (and have used successfully over many years) to help team members deal effectively with the specifics of the conflict and ultimately resolve it.

Finally, we facilitated the team in the use of Lewin's Force Field Analysis tool to analyze their problem and make a decision regarding the most advantageous technology.

This teambuilding intervention occurred over two days, was very intense and resulted in a positive outcome.

### The Implementation Team

Data-gathering and analysis for another teambuilding effort, this one in a large research organization, revealed that the team felt unempowered (actually stymied) due to an autocratic, micromanaging team leader. Their task to implement a new technology companywide had come to a halt.

We were able to use the anonymous data we had gathered to help the team leader understand how his style was negatively affecting the team's behavior and progress. We then coached the leader, one-on-one, behind the scenes, to enhance his leadership skills.

During the actual teambuilding event, we utilized tailored exercises in the Leadership component of the model to help the team understand the utility and necessity of employing shared leadership in order to ensure progress on the project. When working under the Roles/Utilization of Resources model com ponent, we used a roles clarification exercise to establish clear expectations regarding the role contribution of each team member and the team leader. We then exposed the team to Vroom's Model to help them understand under what circumstances unilateral decision making by the team leader was appropriate and when using the team's input (and/or having the team actually make the decision) was most advantageous. The team eventually was very successful in its drive to implementation.

### The Fast-Track Project Team

Recently, we were called in by a well known pharmaceutical firm to assist a large (200-plus members) team to meet some aggressive time lines. This team was charged with taking a potential blockbuster drug through clinical trials to submit a New Drug Application (NDA) to the Food and Drug Administration (FDA). The potential for the drug was so great that the FDA had granted Fast-Track status to facilitate the drug's getting to patients expeditiously. The problem, of course, was that Fast-Track status meant tighter deadlines and ever more resources in the project in order to meet them.

Our data-gathering revealed a number of areas where teambuilding could help. Primary among them was a major communication issue between clinical researchers conducting trials in the field and the project staff at the corporate headquarters. Critical decisions made at headquarters were not always communicated to field researchers, and clinical trial results were being received at corporate late and using inconsistent formats. There was also information indicating that people responsible for tasks near the end of the NDA process weren't aware of or prepared for the new, tighter time lines. We also discovered some serious issues among the team's leadership.

These findings led us to conduct three separate teambuilding sessions—one for the senior team leaders, one for the middle layer of leaders on the team and one for the entire team. This methodology of using "cascading" teambuilding sessions is common in our practice when dealing with larger teams where decisions/direction from the top of the team structure must be broadcast through middle leaders to the entire project team.

With the senior team, we used the model to ensure alignment on direction, time lines (Goals component of the model), role clarity (Roles and Utilization of Resources component) and communication methods/techniques used among themselves and with the rest of the team (Communication component).

With the middle layer of leadership, we cascaded downward the decisions, agreements and expectations developed at the senior level. The middle-layer leaders then reached alignment among themselves and grappled with technical processes and procedures (Controls and Procedures component of the model), which were required to ensure that the new, tighter time lines would be met.

We then assembled the larger, 200-person, team. Once the agreements, decisions and expectations were cascaded downward, they worked in small groups to internalize the new information. They were then challenged to be creative about how they could best flex in order to meet the new time lines (Experimentation and Creativity component of the model). We were able to give them tools to assist in their innovation and creativity. They also made decisions on new procedures for communicating accurate and consistent information in a timely manner.

This team was able to meet its time lines and, in fact, broke all company records in getting an NDA through the process. The drug was recently approved by the FDA and is on track to be the biggest moneymaker ever for this well known pharmaceutical firm.

## *The Executive Team*

The executive leadership team for a large systems integrator firm called us in to assist the team through a major revamping of the company's approach to their business. Our assessment revealed that their organizational structure led to a serious issue with overlapping business lines and customers. This created an internal competition when vying for customer contracts and battles for the company talent and resources needed to successfully meet contract requirements. We also discovered inconsistencies in how various parts of this company bid contracts and how they priced their services.

A three-day teambuilding session led to a reassessment and clarification of the mission/vision of the company and a reorganization among various divisions to better focus on their customer segments. Utilizing every component of the High-Performance Team Model, we were able to facilitate the executive team through some very tough decisions regarding what business they were in, who their customers really were, how to best organize and market to win contracts and how to beat their competition in the customer's eyes.

Long days, intense conversations and use of the model to structure the discussion and decision-making process led to major changes in the company and a more successful business model.

These are just a few examples of how the High-Performance Team Model and methodology were applied to real team challenges. They also illustrate the tangible results that can be achieved.

## Influence of Corporate Culture on Teambuilding

Corporate culture has a strong influence on teams in an organization as well as how they are viewed and supported. We believe that teams and teamwork are an integral part of the work process everywhere, whether it is formally acknowledged or not. The degree to which a corporate culture recognizes the value of teams directly correlates to its support for teambuilding.

Some cultures are very supportive of their teams and encourage proactive teambuilding at their startup as well as intermittent tune-ups as they mature and progress. Many cultures tolerate teambuilding but only if a team is failing or in serious dysfunction. Some do not recognize teambuilding as a viable strategy, no matter what the circumstances, or are only willing to do the very superficial, brief, fun version—and then, only if forced to do so.

Our extensive experience with corporate cultures that are supportive, and even those that tolerate teambuilding when the team is in crisis, reinforces the success that can be achieved with a serious teambuilding strategy. The results we've achieved have influenced even the most skeptical organizations about the merits of our process.

## Summary and Conclusions

Perhaps we have dispelled some myths about teamwork (particularly the one that it is not a natural occurrence!). Since teams are an inherent part of everyday work life, we must develop competencies to ensure successful teams and teamwork. We need to minimize our own and others' frustrations with malfunctioning teams.

We hope we have helped you fully appreciate the importance of a serious teambuilding strategy. We've been privileged to work with hundreds of teams over the past twenty-six years, in a vast variety of industries and circumstances. Our High-Performance Team Model and methodology has proved to be an exciting, valuable tool in helping teams be successful, as illustrated by the examples we presented earlier.

You've also seen how powerful a serious teambuilding process can be. Our normative database provides quantitative results that support the value of our teambuilding approach.

Lastly, we hope we have raised your awareness and expectations about what teambuilding really means. It is, and must be, a far more serious process than what many have experienced to date. It goes far beyond blindfolds and fun get-togethers!

Please recognize the need, importance and value of serious teambuilding. But most importantly, be willing to have an influence and take action!

## About The Authors

### Dr. Jacalyn Sherriton

Dr. Jacalyn Sherriton is President and Founder of Corporate Management Developers and Health Management Consultants, Inc., with offices in Hollywood, Florida, and Reston, Virginia. She founded the companies over twenty-five years ago, and was a pioneer in the organization development field. Jacky specializes in: Creating new or changing corporate cultures toward targeted objectives such as teamwork, service and high performance; Merging corporate cultures and preventing or mitigating culture clash; and Building high performance teams, such as executive, organizational, interdivisional or project teams. Jacky is an executive coach and helps senior leaders adjust and lead in the current dynamic business environment. She provides both a strategic and tactical perspective in addressing organization challenges. Her clients include: ExxonMobil, Capital One, Nabisco, IBM, Campbell Soup, Schering-Plough, SAIC, Bristol-Myers Squibb, The Tribune Corporation, American Security Group, TRW/BDM, Ford, Panasonic, FDA, FAA & DOE to name a few. In addition, Jacky is an accomplished speaker at association conferences such as ASAE, ASTD, HRSP and AMA International Presidents Association. She received the degrees of Bachelor of Science, Magna Cum Laude, from the State University of New York at Buffalo; Master of Education from Boston University; and Doctor of Science from Harvard University. She has been awarded numerous honors, including Outstanding Young Woman of America; Who's Who in the Southeast; Successful Women in Florida; and Doctoral Training Fellowship from Harvard University. Jacky and Jim have published a book, *Corporate Culture/Team Culture,* and have been featured in USA Today, New York Times, CNBC, Entrepreneur Magazine, INC. and Fortune Magazine. Their book has been translated and distributed in China.

**Corporate Management Developers, Inc.**
**Health Management Consultants, Inc.**

200 S. Park Road, Suite 330          1985 B Villa Ridge Drive
Hollywood, FL 33021                      Reston, VA 20191
(954) 961-1663                                (703) 620-0090

E-Mail: consultants@cmd-hmc.com
Website: www.cmd-hmc.com

## James L. Stern

Jim Stern is Vice President and partner in the national consulting firms, Corporate Management Developers and Health Management Consultants, Inc. with offices in Hollywood, Florida, and Reston, Virginia. Jim has over 26 years experience in business and organization development consulting. Jim's many clients include Fortune 500 companies such as ExxonMobil, Capital One, IBM, Nabisco, Universal Health Services, Campbell Soup, Schering-Plough, Bristol-Myers Squibb and Ford. He also has many clients in the public sector including FDA, FAA, DOE, GSA, U.S. Navy, U.S. Air Force and Broward County, FL. Jim's experience, gained over 25 years working with diverse industries, clients, and executives, has made him a specialist in creating, changing and merging "corporate cultures". He is also recognized for his expertise in assisting and building high performance executive, organizational and project teams. Jim is sought after as an executive, one-on-one coach. He works with senior and mid-level executives in providing a structured, practical, results-oriented approach to the coaching experience. Jim holds a Bachelor of Science degree in Business Administration; received his Master of Science degree focusing in Organization Development; and is ABD for a doctorate in Human Resources Development. Jacky and Jim have published a book, *Corporate Culture/Team Culture,* and have been featured in USA Today, New York Times, CNBC, Entrepreneur Magazine, INC. and Fortune Magazine. Their book has been translated and distributed in China.

### Corporate Management Developers, Inc.
### Health Management Consultants, Inc.

<table>
<tr><td>200 S. Park Road, Suite 330</td><td>1985 B Villa Ridge Drive</td></tr>
<tr><td>Hollywood, FL 33021</td><td>Reston, VA 20191</td></tr>
<tr><td>(954) 961-1663</td><td>(703) 620-0090</td></tr>
</table>

E-Mail: consultants@cmd-hmc.com
Website: www.cmd-hmc.com

# Chapter Seven

## It's a Jungle Out There! Team Survival Strategies for Today's Tribes

### Kristi Valenzuela

For millions of Americans, the hottest talk around the water cooler is about the latest dramas on reality TV. Television shows like *The Apprentice* and *Survivor* have captivated us with real-life stress, complex human emotions and traumatic twists in human behavior. From the strong voice of Donald Trump announcing, "You're fired" to *Survivor's* host declaring, "The tribe has spoken" while extinguishing another torch, the result is the same: an individual is sent home as the weakest link of his or her team.

There is no doubt that real life is different from these sixty-minute roller coasters of human trivia and triumph. Our lives are 24-7, without commercial breaks and new seasonal players. However, are there enough similarities between the two to take some teambuilding lessons back to our offices and real-life teams and tribes? Does the prime-time jungle of reality shows really stand in stark contrast to our everyday, competitive jungle where the philosophy is "kill or be killed"?

Fortunately for us, work is not a game of elimination that leaves only one person standing. But many times, there is frustratingly high turnover when trying to find people to fill unique positions for a team, including the leader. Small businesses and global corporations fight to survive and be profitable among their competition every day. There is a constant quest to build strong, competent teams with excellent communication, leadership and follow-through skills. They need great leaders who understand the art of coaching people to be accountable for their individual and team responsibilities.

In the world of high-pressure reality shows, the strategies of outwit, outplay and outlast bring out the good, the bad and the ugly when it comes to leadership and teamwork. Even though some of these tactics are part of the game on TV, these same strategies are often misused intentionally and unintentionally in real-life corporate situations. We can learn from some of these principles and use them to draw parallels to the real world.

## Strategy #1: Choosing a Tribal Leader for the Team

The principle of teambuilding is an intricate balance between the performance of great leaders and motivated team players with the dynamics of communication, follow-through and individual relationships. Refining these key strategies is vital to the productivity of the team and the profitability of the company.

Often, leadership fails when those who are peak performers in their current positions are promoted to higher-level leadership positions without the appropriate leadership training. Unfortunately, even with the best intentions, these individuals are being set up to fail.

Many times, new leaders lack the basic understanding of how teams function and, more importantly, how to obtain individual accountability. The result of this lack of knowledge is frustration not only from the leader but also the entire team.

A great team player does not always make a natural leader. In fact, when people are promoted to take on leadership positions, the survival skills they used to get ahead and get noticed as individuals are contradictory to those needed to be effective leaders. For example, as a team member, it is acceptable to announce your accomplishments in order to get ahead, as long as it is done with integrity. On the other hand, a leader who boasts of his accomplishments can be seen as ungrateful for the work done by the team. This can lead to resentment and rebelliousness within the team. A peak performer team member does not always translate into a strong leader; the skills needed are not parallel. New skills in communication, coaching and motivation need to be learned and incorporated into everyday practices.

Great leaders are results-driven as well as skilled communicators. They are able to put the project and other people before themselves and can motivate each individual to follow through with what he or she is accountable for. They have the ability to share their detailed vision, incorporate team values, and lead the team through breakdowns, while gaining accountability by each individual on the team.

## Strategy #2: Finding Tribal Synergy as the Leader

In order to orchestrate true "tribal synergy"—leading two or more people to achieve one common goal—a leader must have excellent communication skills, patience and an in-depth understanding of the principles of coaching for accountability.

Think of times when you had to ask someone to do something. Were there times when you thought you communicated effectively, even gained a commitment, but the person did not follow through? What happened? Was it a breakdown in self-motivation, communication or leadership skills?

Learning to coach people to stand up for their own greatness is an important learned skill that can assist people in achieving their dreams and staying accountable to promises they make to themselves and to others. In order to coach the tribe and build a strong team, leaders need to understand why people do (or don't do) the things to which they say they are committed.

161

Not only is it frustrating when someone says he is going to do something and subsequently falls short, it can bring a team to a screeching stop. Not only does this slow down productivity but it can cause resentment within the team.

When someone says he is going to do something and doesn't, it boils down to three main principles, all of which are the result of poor communication on the part of the leader, the individual team members or the team as a whole. The survival of a leader depends on understanding these principles and having the ability to coach through the challenge.

**Three reasons why people do not follow through:**
1. They don't understand.
2. They don't take you seriously.
3. They don't see the goal, benefit or payoff.

Let's look at each reason in more detail.

### *They don't understand.*

When discussing a new system, project or idea, it is important to think full-circle. Begin with the objective of why the idea or project is important, and then ask for the team's perception of the concept and why it could be of value to them. Plan the project using a step-by-step process, brainstorming it as a group from start to finish. Creating ownership by everyone involved will establish focus and motivate each individual toward personal accountability. It is important to allow time for questions and answers to explain any concept that is unclear.

Never *assume* that everyone has the same concept of how to carry out the system! Often, people fall into the trap of believing that others should know better or assume that something is commons sense. The truth is that one person's concept of common sense may not be shared by everyone! Common sense is based on each person's individual life experiences, so really there is no such thing as one common sense!

After brainstorming the entire concept from start to finish, quickly debrief everyone's personal responsibility. Ask for each person's individual intention for contribution as well his or her specific goals at final completion. Then ask them how you can support them during the process. You could offer to call or check in with them at specific points prior to their completion date or set up a buddy system for accountability within the team. Share with them that if they get stuck at any point during the project, they must ask for support within twenty-four hours. Finally, ask for any closing questions.

### They don't take you seriously.

This is probably the most frustrating of all the principles. When others don't take you seriously, their reaction is usually based on a past experience. For instance, at some time in the past, you may have asked someone to do something, but that person did not follow through and was never held accountable for the incompletion of the project. Leaders who do not walk the talk of accountability set an unacceptable example.

Usually, if someone does not take the process seriously, he will not speak up and tell you. Instead, he will agree outwardly but in his own mind never have any intention of dedicating himself to carrying out the task.

On the first offense, it is important to *not* make this person appear wrong; he is simply acting based on his past experiences. Instead, coach him by seeking to understand where he is coming from. Then express your concern and seek to have your side understood by the other person. Finally, create a win-win situation by acknowledging the big picture of how the team or the individual will benefit from the final outcome.

If this behavior turns into common practice, it may be time to implement the company guidelines for verbal and written warnings.

### *They don't see the goal, benefit or payoff.*

Leaders carry the biggest mirrors. It is important for the leader of the team to ask a series of questions to understand where a team breakdown may have occurred. Miscommunication and motivation could be playing a major role.

Reevaluate the presentation of the idea, concept or project. Was the information presented in an easy-to-understand, step-by-step, detailed process? Was the information too complicated to implement after leaving the initial meeting? Was there a specific goal and date of completion? Was each person involved in the development of how the project should be carried out? Did each individual share his personal accountability as well as how he and the team could benefit?

Many times, at the preliminary meeting, the final, most important step to creating a productive outcome is missed. That final step is to visualize the goal, understand the benefit, create ownership of the payoff and set a date for completion.

## Strategy #3: Tribal Vision Equals Team Strength

Most of us have experienced disappointment as leaders or team members after delivering what we thought were clear directions. Many times, it's easier to say, "If you want something done right, you have to do it yourself." At the time, they may seem like words of wisdom, but they are probably the result of an unclear vision of what needs to be done. What would life look like if we could produce amazing results every time we had a conversation? In order to accomplish great teamwork, we need to be able to understand the vision and establish the values of our team.

Establishing team vision starts with understanding what is important and developing a solid concept of where the team is going. It is a shared, meaningful description of the direction of the team. It establishes direction, momentum and team commitment. A new vision statement can be developed before taking on a large project, or it can be used as an ongoing team mantra.

To create ownership by the team, it is important to create the vision statement together. Start by calling a team meeting and describing the purpose of the vision statement. Give examples of how vision statements can be used—team mantra, marketing tag line or project direction. A vision statement used as a marketing tag line should say something to the customers about who the company is while at the same time reminding the team of what it stands for. Here are some examples:

### Walt Disney — "We create happiness"

This tells visitors that they will be happy if they visit Walt Disney World or Disneyland. It also reminds the cast members (employees) what they are supposed to accomplish every day.

### Pepperidge Farms — "Never have an ordinary day"

Reminds the consumer and the company that their product is unique and fun.

### Imagine Salon — "The focus is on you...Imagine it"

Shares an important message to salon guests that they will be the center of attention. It also reminds the team members to stay focused.

Creating team values together is another method for helping a team stay focused. It is important for new and existing members alike to reevaluate these values so that they might be enhanced or embraced once again. Call a team meeting and ask each individual to list four professional values that he or she feels are important to the work environment.

1. Honesty
2. Integrity
3. Communication
4. Teamwork
5. Flexibility

6. Fun

7. Professionalism

8. Leadership

9. Follow-through

10. Timeliness

The list above may represent the accumulative list of the team during the meeting. To create ownership of the values have the team vote on their top three values. These values should be used when interviewing new team members, employee meetings, and individual goal setting sessions. These values should be re-visited and reevaluated once a year by the group. As the team grows and changes it is okay for the values to change and other strong values put into place.

## Strategy #4: Get the Tribe Dancing to the Same Drum

In the cutthroat world of reality-show entertainment, motivating others is often manipulative and deceitful. Although this is the opposite of what we need to do in our work lives, learning how to master the art of positively motivating others is essential in business to achieve everyday goals and success.

In order to achieve outstanding results, we must keep in mind that what ignites us as individuals does not necessarily motivate other team members.

The leader and each individual on the team need to understand the intrinsic motivators of other team members. You will move, touch, inspire or enroll others in the possibility of the end result when you can tap into what they are motivated by. Coach Joe Gilliam, a professional career trainer, speaks about the ten intrinsic human motivators on his audio program *The Winner in You: Be Your Own Hero*. His ten motivators are:

1. Achievement—the need to fulfill a goal

2. The need to acquire possessions or wealth

3. The need to affiliate and be accepted by others

4. The need to be independent

5. The need to be creative

6. The need for status
7. The need for power or control
8. The need for recognition
9. The need for safety—avoiding risk and seeking security
10. The need to provide service or give to others

Let's take a more detailed look at each of these. I have interpreted each according to the way a person guided by that motivator might interact with others.

### 1. The need to achieve

These are goal-orientated people. They will lean in, make solid eye contact and ask detailed questions about your desires for a final goal.

### 2. The need for possessions or wealth

These people may share information with others about what they own, what they would like to own and how they plan to do it. They will become very interested in bonuses, if applicable to the project.

### 3. The need to affiliate with others

These people are active in associations, parties, group hobbies, etc. They will be happy to know that they will be involved with other people on the project.

### 4. The need to be independent

These people are self-motivated and like doing things themselves, although they could have a difficult time delegating to others. May be entrepreneurs or prefer a positions where they are in control of how much they can earn or achieve and how quickly they can do it.

### 5. The need to be creative

These people like to think out of the box. They may dress trendily and enjoy coming up with interesting and different ways to do the ordinary. They like guidance but not specific direction.

### 6. The need for status

These people like to climb the ladder of success and compare themself to others in terms of possessions. They become very interested if the project contains the possibility for advancement. They like working on projects with the people they aspire to be like.

### 7. The need for power and control

These people like to be the leader. Body language includes great posture, firm handshake and great eye contact. They speak directly, assertively and with focus. Are quick to delegate, if needed. They remember that power and control are healthy as long as they are not abused.

### 8. The need for recognition

These people like to be acknowledged when projects are completed. No job is too small to be acknowledged. They like to receive thank-you cards, pats on the back or a firm handshake for a job well done.

### 9. The need for safety

These people will play full out, knowing that job security is always present. They may have insecure body language such as avoiding eye contact or asking what-if questions until safety and security are talked about in conversation.

## *10. The need to provide service or give to others*

These people enjoy service-orientated careers or projects. They will be excited to hear that the project involves helping others and how others will be able to benefit.

In his audio presentation, Coach Joe directs listeners to rate these intrinsic motivators on a scale from one to five—one meaning that it doesn't fit at all and five meaning that it fits well. After listeners have rated the motivators, they are to list the three that seem to describe them the best. This is an amazing self-discovery process that can be used by a team to discover what motivates each individual the most.

I have used this exercise effectively in teambuilding atmospheres. I like to go a step further by discovering the top three that motivate the team as a whole. I have found the most common team motivators to be:

1. The need for recognition
2. The need for achievement
3. The need for service

Tapping into a team's top three intrinsic motivators will assist in understanding how to communicate, reward and inspire the group. It will also open up the possibility for clear, productive communication. If your team rates recognition as one of its top motivators, then designating an employee of the month or publishing acknowledgment in a company newsletter can be great motivators. If achievement ignites them, create ways they can earn bonuses, time off or specialized titles for their accomplishments.

Mastering the art of motivation will create a winning, exciting environment, produce amazing results in remarkable time and eliminate defeating frustration!

## Strategy #5 Avoid Tribal Breakdowns...go by the book!

You can count on the natives getting restless when there is a breakdown in tribal synergy and team working systems. Before you find out who your head hunters are, make sure you are setting your team up for success with solid training systems and company guidelines. Top companies in the world have built their brand and success by utilizing detailed training manuals.

Let's take a look at some of the top tribes of the customer service/sales world, Victoria's Secret, Outback, Bath and Body Works, and the king of the jungle of them all... Disney World. What do they all have in common? They are all profitable, nationally and internationally recognized, well-branded companies with strong company vision, and values. They demand specific standards from their team, and have foundational training to set them up for success. They have black and white guidelines for customer service, sales, and teamwork.

In a world where only the strongest survive, what separates the rulers of the jungle from the others? Consistency, follow through, and dedication to the systems. They all have great trainers, step-by-step systems, and a foundational detailed Team Training Manual to guide their way.

A team-training manual assists these top companies in implementing their specific standards in a uniform way to enable their brand and uniqueness to shine. It assists their managers in training, and even disciplinary actions. Perhaps this is why we will never see Snow White smoking a cigarette in the 5:00 parade, or ever witness Mini Mouse telling off Mickey Mouse in front of the Magic Kingdom. Cast members at Disney are extensively trained in customer service, any veering from the guidelines, and they are quickly asked to go play somewhere else.

Set your team up for SUCCESS! Creating a detailed team manual or playbook is essential to a building a strong team. It will help define your unique "brand", company vision, and team values. It is the reference tool when hiring, training, and growing team members.

Here is an outline of topics that top companies include in their manuals...

- Mission statement & Core values
- Interviewing procedures & Exit interview procedures
- Training and Orientation guidelines
- Job Descriptions
- Policies & Procedures
- Scripting for speaking with customers
- Systems to Increase Profitability
- Management Responsibilities
- Handling Angry Clients
- Evaluations & Disciplinary Actions
- Team Evaluations
- Strategies to Advance within the Company

**FREE Demo Software Offer! Create your own manual!**

One of the biggest challenges we have heard from company owners is they don't have time to organize, create, type, and produce an extensive manual for their team. Not to worry, that is our specialty! We have studied the leaders doing it right in customer service and sales, and have developed a unique employee training manual specific to the Customer Service and Sales Industry. Not only does the manual include the necessary foundational principles of every employee handbook such as sexual harassment, sick time and timeliness, it also includes tips on interviewing, hiring and training, and "how to" systems for customer service and retailing. The team-training manual is also accompanied by software which allows companies to easily add their company name, and customize the step-by-step systems to fit their needs. Contact us for your FREE DEMO Software 1.877.378.8212.

## Strategy #6 Positive, Productive Tribal Council Meetings

One of the most important survival strategies for today's jungle is excellent tribal communication. Meetings are essential to keep everyone updated on current strategies, upcoming events, and to celebrate successes since the last tribal council. Many times owners, and management become frustrated due to low meeting attendance, losing control of the "classroom", with rude or out of turn speaking, or simply that meetings never seem to resolve challenges, or seem productive.

### *Let's look at the common challenges:*

- Poor Attendance
- Meeting starts late and ends late
- Problems are brought up
- No solutions are offered to resolve problems
- Negativity
- Getting off track
- Rude, or out of turn speaking
- Lack of follow through

Anything you do on a consistent basis you need a system. This is true for tribal meetings also. A detailed agenda, and simple classroom/teacher skills can help keep meetings civilized, productive, and positive.

Let's take a look at systems and solutions for each of the above challenges...

*Poor Attendance:* Many team members will skip out on tribal meetings because the meetings are usually negative, and there may not be a consequence if the meeting is missed. Solution: Create a detailed guideline regarding meetings, explain the importance of meeting attendance during interview process, and be clear on any consequences of missed meetings.

Have a sign up list in the break room for those who will be attending the meeting, along with request forms to miss the meeting. On the request form provide an area where the employee must write out their excuse for being absent for the upcoming meeting, along with an area for the manager to approve, or not approve. These should be filed in the employee's history file.

***Leader starts late, and runs longer than promised:*** Many team members will purposely come to the meeting 5 – 10 minutes late due to the poor history of the meeting leader always starting late. Solution: Always start meetings on time even if there is only one person there at "go time". Always end when promised even if there are still things on your agenda. Plan a second meeting date, or send the remaining information in the form of a memo.

***Problems with no solutions:*** It frustrates everyone when problems are brought up at a meeting, and the meeting takes a negative turn. Rarely are un-planned problems resolved during the meeting, and usually casue the meeting to get off track. Solution: All problems to be discussed at the meeting must be in writing and brought to the manager prior to the meeting. Also, there must be two solutions in writing by the individual submitting the challenge. The leader can then pre-plan a brainstorming exercise for the group, or handle the challenge outside of the meeting.

***Getting off track:*** Just like any great speaker or classroom teacher for any meeting there needs to be a pre-planned agenda, or curriculum. Meetings lose control due to poor pre-planning. Solution: Create a detailed agenda and time line for each segment of the meeting. Review the agenda with the team at the beginning of the meeting so each person is aware of the content that needs to be covered. Let them know they can ask questions after the meeting if you need to move on to the next item on the agenda to stay on time.

***Rude or out of turn speaking:*** Side conversations can begin when team members are bored, are passionate about the topic, or when other members are speaking. Solution: Set the guidelines before the meeting of speaking out of turn let them know the timeliness of the meeting depends on attention, and being respectful when others are talking. Use a "talking stick" or an item to pass to the person speaking. Only the person with the "tribal idol" can speak.

***Lack of follow through:*** Meetings often seem like wasted time when there is lack of follow through after the meeting is over. Solution: Gain team and individual commitments before the meeting is adjourned. Spend the last 5 minutes of every meeting with a commitment exercise. Have each individual write down the team's responsibilities and deadlines along with their personal accountabilities and dates. Go around the room and have each person announce their individual commitment to the project. Collect these written commitments and follow up on achievements after the meeting.

### Strategy #7 - Evaluation of Individual Tribal Commitments

Tribal upset can occur when team members feel that someone is not holding up to their personal accountabilities. A quarterly self-evaluation and tribe evaluation keeps everyone on his or her toes. Beware, with this system, slackers don't stay. If you want to build a team of peak performers, this tool could be right for you.

**Self-evaluation / Co-worker Evaluation:** This self-evaluation and co-worker evaluation is used as a learning tool and it assists in setting valuable personal goals. This keeps tribe members aware of their daily actions, knowing that they will have to review themselves, and their team members will be reviewing them every 90-days.

The evaluations should consist of your core values and what you have established as great customer service with in your business. The principles on the form should be simple along with a rating scale from 1-10. All tribe members rate themselves and each other on established values. All tribe members will get a copy of total rating from team members and one copy will be posted to their personnel file.

| Evaluated Area | Rate 1 – 10 (see key, below) |
|---|---|
| Timeliness (arrival & breaks) | |
| Interaction with clients and co-workers | |
| Attitude: smile, body language, verbal | |
| Organization: cleanliness, neatness of area | |
| Professional, consistent, friendly | |
| Teamwork: offering help beyond expected duties | |
| Daily duties | |
| Communication: honest, clear, professional, non-gossip | |
| Exceeding expectations – clients | |
| Personal Appearance | |

**Key:**
**1 – 2 Unacceptable**: will not, does not, avoids, or has great difficulty with.
**3 – 4 Needs Improvement:** shows limited effort, infrequently practices.
**5 – 6 Meets Standards:** knows and uses, readily practices, meets team standards.
**7 – 8 Above Average:** easily performs, exhibits leadership, above team standards.
**9 – 10 Exceeds Expectations:** Wow factor, exceptional leadership with co-workers and clients.

Defining your winning team strategies can build a strong, lean tribe for today's jungle. Using these strategies will help you outwit, outplay, and outlast your competition, and will assist you in creating a tribal culture with focused values, and tribal synergy.

## About The Author

### Kristi Valenzuela

Kristi is an International Speaker, Success Coach and Author, and is the founder of Team Path Educational Systems a division of Crystal Focus Coaching. Team Path Educational Systems focuses on "People skills for profitability." The company offers team training manuals, audios and other interactive support tools. Kristi has coached thousands of professionals nationally and internationally, helping them achieve their personal and career goals. She consistently earns rave reviews for her "real" systems and solutions, through interactive and energetic presentations along with training tools. Kristi has been featured or quoted in several magazines, and has been a guest on SkyRadio, broadcasting to 5.2 million listeners. Kristi is a professional member of the National Speakers Association and has quickly gained international recognition in several industries as one of the top business strategy and motivational speakers. Kristi's most requested programs specialize in providing simple; fun and easy solutions for common teambuilding challenges including topics on teamwork, retailing, front desk systems, marketing and team accountability. Kristi knows the secrets of success and profitability. She believes... "SUCCESS IS EASY WHEN YOUR TEAM KNOWS HOW!"

**Kristi Valenzuela, President**
Crystal Focus, Inc.
Team Path Educational Systems
202 Astor Knolls Drive
Ortonville, MI  48462
Tel: 1.877.378.8212
Fax: 248.627.2267
Email: kvzuela@aol.com
www.teampathsystems.com

# Chapter Eight

## Balancing the Scales of
## Team Leadership

### Lee S. Johnsen

"I wonder what's up," Dane Franklin thought to himself as he scanned the e-mail from his boss, Marie, asking him to meet in her office the next morning at 8:00 a.m. sharp.

Five years earlier, Dane had joined Midwestern Bank and Commerce (MBC), one of the top regional banking firms in the Midwest, as a collections supervisor and after three years was promoted to collections manager when his predecessor retired. He had achieved some nice successes during his tenure with MBC and could not imagine that Marie was anything but happy with his work. He had improved the collections ratios for the team he first supervised and had served on the company task force to upgrade the technology systems. From his work on the task force, he was exposed to managers from other divisions and caught the attention of the senior management sponsor for the task force, who later asked Dane to serve on the HR Policy Review Committee. From these opportunities, Dane had earned the reputation of having a solid knowledge of collections and of being an innovative thinker and a team player.

He knew the e-mail couldn't be bad news about his performance.

Neither could he imagine that his company was in trouble. Midwestern Bank and Commerce—whose regional headquarters in Sioux Falls, South Dakota, his home base—was a healthy corporation with 500 employees in Sioux Falls and another 800 scattered among the fifty branch offices in South Dakota, Kansas, Minnesota and Nebraska. Over its seventy-year existence the bank had weathered the Depression, the farm crisis of the 1980s and myriad ups and downs. It was once again on the upswing—no small feat given the highly competitive banking environment in which mergers and acquisitions were becoming commonplace. MBC was always able to change with the times and expand its markets beyond the traditional agricultural customers who had been its original mainstay.

As Dane arrived at Marie's office the next morning, he found her already steeped in paperwork. Raised on the prairies of South Dakota, Marie Stiner, vice president of operations, was proud of her sense of independence and widely respected for her uncommon ability to get things done. Despite the doubts of others, she had proven herself in a business in which the "good ol' boy" heritage was alive and well. Equally uncommon was her seemingly innate ability to coach her staff. Under Marie's leadership, operations efficiency had improved fifty percent in the last three years, bringing significant dollars to the bank's bottom line. Marie was a key player at the bank and maintained a good working relationship with the company president, Darrell Bergstrom. She was often called upon to make things happen when new initiatives needed a senior-management sponsor.

"What's up Marie?" Dane queried as he sat down in the chair across from her desk. "Dane, I'll get right to the point," Marie said, not missing a beat. "Our strategy document this year states that one of our strategic initiatives for the next two years is to improve our ailing customer service. While the new technology systems have helped, our current customer service ratings stink." Dane knew that Marie wasn't one to mince words, but even he was taken back by her candor.

"As you know, service excellence is critical to our growth," she continued. "I've been asked to serve as a senior-management sponsor for a team that will be charged with creating a strategy and system to improve our service delivery company-wide. The team will be made up of representatives from several departments, including our branch offices, and will present its recommendations to the entire Senior Management Group on December 19th. Dane, I'd like you to head up this team."

Dane sat back in his chair, his head spinning. December 19th was just a little more than six months away, and his schedule as collections manager was already strained. He had reviewed the strategy document briefly but hadn't realized the situation was this serious or that senior management was willing to give it this kind of attention. Before he could begin to put words to his concerns, Marie went on. "Dane, you've done a great job of working with your team of collections supervisors and made real progress in reducing our delinquencies. You were also a key member of the Technology Implementation Team and have experience working with other departments. This will be a new opportunity for you that no doubt will stretch you and the others on your team. I know that leading a team like this is not the same as your Collections Team leadership experience, but I am confident you are ready for this assignment. It will require a good deal of your time, and, unfortunately, I can't take you out of your current role as collections manager. However, as the team sponsor, I will be there to support you. I can help you reassign some of your day-to-day duties among your staff. That will be a good growth opportunity for them, too. What do you say?"

"This does sound exciting. I'm interested," Dane replied. "But are you sure I'm the right person? It is a pretty big stretch for me."

"If I weren't sure, do you think I'd be talking to you about this?" Marie quipped. "I suspect your occasional absences from your supervisors could teach them to function a bit more independently, which is what we would expect given their background and experience. As I said, I'll help you and your team and work with the other senior managers to clarify their expectations and support your efforts. We have high hopes for your team. We need this group to hit a home run, both to regain our customer service reputation and to improve profitability, and I'm convinced that you can provide the leadership to make that happen."

"Okay, I'll do it," Dane agreed. "When and how do we get started?"

"You can start by reading this project overview from the Senior Management Group and opening up some time on your calendar," Marie indicated. "The other team members will be contacted by their managers as soon as I notify them that you've agreed to serve as team leader. By the end of next week, you can hold your first team meeting. Any questions?" she asked.

"Not right now," Dane replied, "but I'm sure I'll have many over the days ahead."

"Fine," said Marie. "Let's meet on Thursday morning and go over them. I will talk to you then about what will make this team different from others you've been involved in. Let's plan to meet at 9:00 a.m." With that, Marie returned to her paperwork, and Dane knew their time was up.

Once Dane returned to his office, he downed a cup of strong coffee and read through the document Marie had handed him.

## Midwestern Bank and Commerce

### Service Excellence Overview

The Situation:

In the highly competitive financial services industry, service is becoming an increasingly critical differentiator to customers. Even customers who rate service as "above average" may leave if they perceive that another provider offers better service. While MBC's commitment to its customers has always been high, service ratings have fallen in recent years. Despite the improvements from technology enhancements, customer survey responses indicate a decline in their satisfaction.

Additionally, increasing the number of bank products owned by our customers is a key component of our long-term growth and profitability strategy. There is an immediate need to conduct both a thorough analysis of current customer service practices and to identify innovative solutions for improving service at MBC.

The Response:

Create a cross-functional team to develop a two-year strategy for improving service delivery.

The Charge:

A cross-functional team, formed in early June, will be charged with creating an organization-wide strategy for improving service delivery. This team will be charged with analyzing best service-delivery practices, comparing them to current organizational practices and developing a comprehensive system for delivering service excellence. This strategy that will support our cultural value and mission of providing the very best in service and products to our customers.

The outputs expected from this team are:

- ◆ Create clear links between customer service excellence and company profitability that can be measured concretely.
- ◆ Enhance the service culture of MBC by defining the elements of great service, establishing measurable service standards on which to base performance and creating a program to recognize employee efforts.
- ◆ Increase employee and supplier awareness of the connections between service excellence and their roles in the organization.
- ◆ Identify key tactics to be applied organization-wide to improve service delivery at company headquarters and branch offices.

The Deadline:

The Service Excellence Team will present their findings and recommendations to the Senior Management Group on December 19th.

When Dane finished reading the overview, he puzzled over Marie's comment that this team would be different from the other teams of which he'd been a part. He was already feeling good about the results his Collections Team had achieved under his leadership, and as a member of the HR Policy Review Board, he already knew how to operate within a group that created companywide policy. "I'll have to ask Marie what she meant by that when we meet on Thursday," he noted to himself. Then he considered the issue of his schedule crunch. "This project is going to be interesting, but I don't know how I'll ever lead a team and do my current job, even with Marie's help," he reflected. Just as he jotted down this question, one of Dane's supervisors arrived at his door with a collections issue, and for the rest of the day, Dane turned his attention to his immediate job without further thought of the new team commitment.

Thursday morning arrived cool and clear, so typical of South Dakota weather in June. While Dane had loved the warm climate in Tucson, where he grew up, and in California, where he attended college, he had come to appreciate all four seasons when his career brought him to the Midwest. "Spring is still my favorite time of year," he thought as he arrived at the office. Having prepared a list of questions, he was ready for his meeting with Marie and was anxious to get his new team together and get started. The team presentation to the Senior Management Group in wintry December would come all too soon.

Marie met Dane at her office door and ushered him into the adjoining conference room. "We'll have more room to spread out in here," she said. "This will be a working meeting, and I want to make sure we cover all the items on both of our agendas."

As they settled into their chairs, Marie continued: "I have some good news, Dane. We have completed the slate of members for your team. If there had been more time, we would have involved you in this, but I've found that team member selection is often overemphasized. What's most important is to find a balance of three categories of skills among team members. A team like this needs to have the right mix of technical and functional skills, problem-solving skills and interpersonal skills. Your fellow team members have those as well as a real desire to be a part of this initiative. Now don't assume that everyone is proficient in all the skills your team might need. But most people can develop the needed skills after joining the team. This will be a great group of people to work with, and with your leadership, I have high hopes. The team includes six other employees representing the marketing, customer service, human resources, finance and credit departments in the home office as well as a branch manager in Kansas. The members have varied backgrounds, tenure and experience with the company, but every one of them is considered an expert in his or her field—bright and willing to take risks. And they all believe in customer service as a business strategy."

"You said that this team would be different from others I've been a part of," Dane remarked. "What do you mean by that? I've already worked with a variety of teams both at work and in community service clubs."

Marie turned in her chair. "Dane," she asked, "do you remember seeing the balance scale in my office—the one on my credenza?"

"Yes, I've noticed it," Dane replied, "and I've wondered why you have it."

"That balance scale," said Marie, "represents what I've learned about the different types of teams. I think it's important for you to gain the same understanding if you are to successfully lead the Service Excellence Team.

"Let me explain," she continued. "There are three types of teams—actually two types of teams and a third that's called Effective Work Groups. Think of **Effective Work Groups** as the base of the balance scale. The base represents a small group that brings together individuals to draw on their collective input and insights. These groups often review recommendations and make policy or other organizational decisions. Frequently, members collaborate to share information and to help each other with their individual areas of responsibility. Effective Work Groups represent teams at the most basic level. Typically, this sort of group never really has a clear mandate of performance goals that requires mutual accountability and commitment. Think about the HR Policy Board that you served on or one of your community clubs. While these groups serve their purposes, they don't have the same kind of focused, measurable performance and results expectations that we have in our department and cross-functional teams."

## BALANCING THE SCALES OF TEAM LEADERSHIP

Work Group and Team Types

Single-Leader Teams     Shared-Leadership Teams

Effective Work Groups

"Effective Work Group members collaborate to establish key disciplines and actions for their leaders and members. These disciplines are important in that they represent a set of principles around which the members agree to operate in order to achieve their purpose. For instance, the HR Policy Board is very effective in analyzing trends and making policy recommendations to the Senior Management Group. Their work helps us to retain our employees and ensure that they are treated fairly, which helps us remain an attractive employer in this area. But Effective Work Groups don't produce the kind of business results needed to stay competitive and to excel. That's where the two trays on the scale come in."

"So what's the difference between an Effective Work Group and the other two kinds of teams?" Dane asked.

"The primary difference," Marie asserted, "is the clarity of the group's focus on performance results and the focus on the appropriate discipline required by the performance challenge." Dane looked puzzled. "Think of your team of collections supervisors," she explained. "I would refer to them as a **Single-Leader Team**. On the scale, a Single-Leader Team sits on one side of the balance. Single-Leader Teams are characterized by having a formal leader who is in control and responsible for the direction and success of the team. The discipline of a Single-Leader Team is defined as the sum of separate, individual contributions directed and managed by a single leader. Often, the leader consults with team members, but it is the *leader* who determines the performance-based reason and purpose for the team, determines who makes the decisions, establishes the required individual contributions and group pattern of communications, determines the requirements of success and decides how and when to evaluate progress. While the team members have certain roles and actions, they are primarily determined by the work to be done and decisions the leader makes."

Dane shifted in his seat as Marie went on. "Think about the work your supervisors do," she continued. "Do they really need each other in order to be successful in their roles? When they set goals for the year, is that not primarily an individual exercise with you and not the collective work of the entire team?"

"Well, yes," conceded Dane, "but what's wrong with that?"

"Nothing!" Marie emphasized. "Whenever a small group can deliver performance through the combined sum of individual contributions, then the Single-Leader Team discipline is the most effective choice. The choice is fast, efficient and comfortable since most organizations have used the single-leader model for years. With this type of team and your leadership approach with them, Dane, the team has been very successful in reducing delinquencies and in improving their efficiency."

"So what will be different about the Service Excellence Team?" asked Dane.

"I'm glad you asked," Marie replied, leaning forward. "This is really important, so pay attention. The work required of the Service Excellence Team is greater than the sum of the individual contributions of its members. The work requires a **Shared-Leadership Team**. A Shared-Leadership Team is on the other side of the scale. It is described as a small number of people with complementary skills who are committed to a common purpose, performance goals and approach. This team discipline demands mutual accountability. All team members, not just the leader, establish the required individual and collective contributions and pattern of communications. The team sets the criteria for success and determines when to evaluate progress. And the team, not the individuals, either succeeds or fails."

"This sounds more complicated than I thought," Dane remarked.

"It is," said Marie. "But when performance demands collective work products of the type your team will be producing, through real-time collaboration and integration of multiple skills and perspectives, the single-leader approach will underperform. That's why you need to understand the differences in the types of teams and the disciplines of each. To help you get started, I'll share with you a reference guide that I have describing group and team types, the disciplines of each and how the actions by the team leader and team members are different, based on the group or team type. The information comes from the extensively researched books by Jon Katzenbach and Douglas Smith, *The Wisdom of Teams* and *The Discipline of Teams*. So get yourself copies. These are great resources for anyone who works with teams. Study this reference guide. We'll talk about it prior to your first team meeting next week."

With that, Marie stood up and said, "Follow the disciplines for Shared-Leadership Teams and you'll be off to a great start when you meet with your team. Then send me an e-mail and let me know how the meeting went." She then handed Dane the following reference guide and left for her next meeting.

# Work Group and Team Types—Descriptions, Disciplines and Actions

| Effective Work Groups |
|---|

**Description:** Commonly known as committees, boards or advisory groups, Effective Work Groups draw on the collective input and insights of their members to make policy decisions, review recommendations and make organizational decisions. Frequently, members collaborate to share information, make decisions and help individual members with their individual areas of responsibility. However, they often do not have a clear mandate of performance goals that requires mutual accountability and commitment. Effective Work Groups are characterized by the following disciplines and actions:

## Disciplines

1. A charter—a document that describes the group's purpose and reasons for working together.
2. Effective communication—members must communicate and coordinate to engage everyone's participation.
3. Clear roles and areas of responsibility—established so that members can work individually or collectively as needed.
4. Time-efficient team procedures—to minimize wandering discussions and wasted time.
5. A sense of accountability—to both individual and collective group accomplishments.

| Leader Actions | Member Actions |
|---|---|
| 1. Lead the group to create a charter if one is not already established and ensure that members adhere to charter guidelines. | 1. Develop an understanding of the group's purpose and offer ideas that deepen their sense of shared purpose and goals. |
| 2. Coordinate communication and encourage information sharing among group members to support the group's purpose. | 2. Share information and ideas among members that support accomplishments of the group's goals. |

| | |
|---|---|
| 3. Clarify roles and responsibilities among group members. Secure new members and resources as needed. | 3. Complete individual responsibilities and offer information and support to other team members. |
| 4. Chair group meetings and monitor group standards so that work processes run smoothly. | 4. Suggest ways to improve the group's work processes to improve effectiveness and efficiency. Offer to create standards where none exist. |
| 5. Model accountability and commitment to achieving the group's goals. Reward and recognize individual and group accomplishments. | 5. Commit to completing individual responsibilities and to contributing to the group's collective goals. |

**Single-Leader Teams**

**Description:** The Single-Leader Team revolves around one leader. The formal leader is in control and responsible for the direction and success of the team. This team discipline is defined as the sum of separate, individual contributions directed and managed by one leader. Often in consultation with team members, the leader determines the performance-based reason and purpose for group work, makes the decisions, establishes the required individual contributions and pattern of communications, determines the requirements of success and decides how and when to evaluate progress. Single-Leader Teams are characterized as follows.

**Disciplines**

1. Individual goals and outputs that add up to the team's purpose.
2. Members work mostly on individual goals and tasks that match their skills.
3. Work products (outcomes) are mostly individual.
4. Leader-driven working approach.
5. Strong individual accountability and commitment.

| Leader Actions | Member Actions |
|---|---|
| 1. Make and communicate decisions for the group. While consultation can be a part of the decision process, the leader makes the final decision. | 1. Participate in team decisions when it is requested by the leader. |
| 2. Set the performance goals and determine individual responsibilities. The leader has the final say about what constitutes an appropriate goal for each member as well as for the team as a whole. | 2. Participate in setting goals with the leader by suggesting individual and team goals and taking responsibility for goals that fit within scope of responsibility. |
| 3. Set the pace and determine the working approach. The leader monitors the progress and pace of each person's effort and motivates individuals as well as the team as a whole. The leader accelerates or slows the pace by setting deadlines for the team and its members. | 3. Accomplish work within the pace and time frames established by the leader. Self-monitor progress in order to meet deadlines. |
| 4. Evaluate the results. The leader is responsible for achieving team results that are acceptable to higher-level managers. The leader recognizes and rewards the contributions and results of individuals. | 4. Evaluate performance compared to individual goals and participate with the leader in evaluating results. May be involved in evaluating team goals at the discretion of the leader. |
| 5. Establish benchmarks and standards. The leader fosters sharing of ideas among the members and encourages best practices both within and outside the team. The leader makes the final decision of the best standards for the group. | 5. Share ideas and best practices among team members in order to improve individual and team efficiency and effectiveness against standards. |

| | |
|---|---|
| 6. Maintains control of the team effort by clarifying individual accountability and emphasizing consequence management. Consequently, team members are clear about their roles, specific goals, expected end products and deadlines. | 6. Focus on individual goals, results, interactions with others and the leader's evaluation of performance. |

## Shared-Leadership Teams

**Description:** A Shared-Leadership Team is a small number of people with complementary skills who are committed to a common purpose, performance goals and approach for which they hold themselves mutually accountable. The team determines the performance rationale and purpose for their work and establishes the required individual and collective contributions. The team also sets the criteria for success and how and when to evaluate progress. Shared-Leadership Teams are characterized by the following disciplines and actions.

### Disciplines

1. A compelling performance purpose that exceeds the sum of individual goals.
2. Members work jointly to integrate complementary talents and skills.
3. Work products (outcomes) are mostly collective or joint efforts.
4. Adaptable working approach shaped and enforced by members.
5. Mutual and individual accountability.

| Leader Actions | Member Actions |
|---|---|
| 1. Intervene only when team members are incapable or unwilling to reach a decision. | 1. Fully participate in decision making based on the individual and collective skills of all team members. Decisions are made by those the team believes are best positioned to do so, based on talent, skill, experience and assigned work task. |

| | |
|---|---|
| 2. Participate in goal setting as a member of the team. This process differs from the characteristic one-on-one negotiation between each member and the leader in Single-Leader Teams. | 2. Collaborate in setting individual and team goals. Goals are not set until team members have explored the implications, weighed the tradeoffs and generated a shared understanding and mutual sense of commitment. The number and value of collective goals invariably outweigh the number and value of individual goals. |
| 3. Contribute suggestions as to pace and working approach and participate in decision making by the team. The leader participates in the real work of the team by performing individual and team tasks that contribute to the team's goals. | 3. Participate in setting the pace and working approach, making these a matter of shared commitment. The team chooses the best way to distribute and integrate work, manage logistics and administration, and establish and enforce norms. The roles and contributions of the members shift to fit different performance-related tasks. |
| 4. Facilitate discussions about individual and shared accountability. Ultimately, these are determined by all team members. | 4. Assess progress against team goals and purpose. When teams evaluate progress, the dialogue is open, nonhierarchical and more focused on performance progress and the entire effort of the team than on individual performance. |
| 5. Contribute actively to identifying a common group purpose and performance goals. Often, the leader serves as the key link among the team, its sponsor and upper management. | 5. Set high standards. These demanding standards arise from a compelling performance purpose to which all members are committed. It is not uncommon for a team to establish a set of goals that exceeds those set in its charter. |

It was June 19th when the Service Excellence Team held its first meeting. That day was particularly memorable for Dane, not only because of the excitement about getting the team together for the first time but also because it was his 35th birthday.

Dane studied the material Marie had given him and was becoming more familiar with the disciplines of Shared-Leadership Teams and how the leaders' and members' roles and actions were indeed different from Single-Leader Teams. The team members represented departments across the company: Kathy, a marketing research analyst; Rex, customer service supervisor; Marchelle, human resource generalist; Kris, credit supervisor; Neoma, senior finance analyst; and Mary Ann, a branch manager in Kansas City. They would be a team of seven, taking on one big challenge for the company.

During the first few weeks, the team met regularly and spent time clarifying the charge given them by the Senior Management Group. They identified specific goals and time frames they needed to achieve to be ready for the December 19th presentation. This was initially difficult, because everyone seemed to have a different idea of what the team should focus on. People weren't used to spending time gaining a common understanding and consensus, and a few people had a tendency to go off on their own or have side conversations. Dane's leadership skills were indeed tested as he and the team worked through these issues together. While getting agreement wasn't easy, once they had it, their team seemed to pull together. At that point, the tasks seemed to naturally fall to those most skilled in dealing with them. Whenever a new task or process came up that no one had experience with, the team decided who should best tackle it and offered their support. It was interesting to watch the roles and contributions shift among the members to fit the performance tasks required.

By September, the team seemed well on its way. Both Dane and Marie were pleased with the team's progress. But then, like a South Dakota wind, the direction of things began to change. Kris, who had been working closely with Kathy to gather the customer survey data essential to creating the links between customer service and profitability, was offered a job by another firm that he felt he couldn't refuse. Within three weeks, he left the team and company. Even though Neoma stepped in to take Kris's place, she had a lot to learn to gain the same level of knowledge Kris had, which meant a delay in the performance standards work she was doing. And it would be another two weeks before Joseph, Kris's replacement, could join the team. Other team members were feeling the strain of managing their regular jobs while also devoting time to the team, and their managers weren't always supportive. Rex was late completing his assignments, and other team members were reluctant to talk to him about it. Mary Ann shared that she felt increasingly separated from the rest of the team when her only connection with them was by phone. Without question, though, the biggest concern was that the team was falling behind in meeting its goals and deadlines. With less than three months before the recommendations were due, the team had only completed forty percent of its work.

Dane wasn't looking forward to stepping into Marie's office for his next meeting, knowing she would ask her usual, "How's it going?" He knew that she knew the team was behind, but he also knew that she would want to hear him talk about it before she offered an opinion. As he entered her office, he took a deep breath and began: "Marie, I'd hoped I'd never have to tell you this, but I'm worried about the team. I'm sure you know we're behind schedule and the members are discouraged. Tensions are high, and some members are even beginning to question whether this is all worth it. They're hearing grumblings from their managers about all the time they're spending with the team that takes them away from their current jobs. We also could use another PC."

"What do you suggest?" Marie inquired calmly.

Dane hesitated and then proceeded, "I think we need some sort of teambuilding event to boost the team's morale and fire them up again. Maybe some communications training would help us to give and receive feedback more effectively. That might ease some of the tension and get us focused again. We could also use a couple more team members to help us catch up on our deadlines. And we definitely need another PC."

"Dane," Marie responded, "let me start by saying that all teams run into problems. That's normal and to be expected whenever you have a group of people who are working hard to accomplish something important. Secondly, the problems you have cited are not really problems at all; they're symptoms of something much deeper that's going on with the team. Thirdly, and this one is the most important, you and your team are ultimately accountable for getting back on track. I can't do it for you and neither can anyone else. Once the team has gotten back on track, they'll have the confidence and commitment to perform far beyond what they've already experienced.

"Now I have good news and bad news," she continued. "The bad news is that we will not be adding any additional members to your team, and the December 19th date for your presentation is firm. The good news is that I will speak to the other senior managers and ask them to reinforce their support of the team's work to your team members' managers. That should take some of the pressure off there. I will also see that you get an additional PC. The other piece of good news is that I have a resource that may be able to help you and your team get back on track. I want you to give him a call and meet with him. But before I give you his name, let me reaffirm this: Without question, the team is responsible for getting itself back on track and meeting the performance challenge they have before them." With that, Marie handed Dane the business card of Vance King, a performance consultant.

Within two days, Vance King was in Dane's office. A man in his mid-forties, Vance had an engaging style and quick wit. Dane found himself surprised at how comfortable he felt as they exchanged pleasantries. Vance shared that he had worked with Marie on several occasions, first as an internal consultant when they were both at a bank in San Diego, and then periodically as an external consultant when he began his own business five years earlier. Now that they were both back in the Midwest, it was easier to keep up with each other's careers.

"So what's a performance consultant, and why does Marie think I need one?" Dane asked. He thought Marie's bluntness must be rubbing off on him. "Well," said Vance, "I can answer the first question, but you'll have to answer the second one. Performance consultants work with their clients to assess a performance need or problem, recommend possible interventions, design and deliver those interventions if needed and then evaluate the impact of the interventions. Intervention is just a term used to describe a variety of solutions designed to improve individual and team performance. Let me give you this handout I've made, which describes the performance consulting process and presents some examples of interventions a performance consultant might use to help individuals and teams improve their performance." Vance handed Dane the following document:

## The Performance Consulting Process
1. Probe to assess performance gaps and their causes
2. Report findings and make recommendations
3. Identify appropriate interventions
4. Deliver interventions
5. Evaluate interventions and their impact on performance

## Performance Interventions

| Intervention: | Used to: | Resulting in: |
| --- | --- | --- |
| Self or team assessments | gain feedback to help the team and its members monitor performance and take corrective actions if necessary. | quicker and more effective responses to performance issues. These responses can maintain and even boost team productivity by focusing on those items having the greatest impact on performance. |

| Intervention: | Used to: | Resulting in: |
| --- | --- | --- |
| Planning workshop | create or update team charters, purpose statements, goals, working approaches and performance measures. | a clearer focus on outputs/work products; improved work processes and approach that increase team productivity and performance. |
| Facilitated discussion | address issues related to team member attitudes, commitment and the team disciplines. | increased team member commitment, energy and collective team performance. |
| Work processes and communications documentation | maintain consistency in outputs as team members' roles change and as team membership changes. | consistent productivity and quality of outputs; improved efficiency and service delivery. |
| Job aids or quick-reference guides | reduce reliance on memory and assist team members in applying consistent practices/responses to repetitive work processes and tasks. | consistent delivery of service and work outputs that meet or exceed defined standards and measures. |
| Training | fill gaps in technical, problem-solving, decision making or interpersonal skills such as listening, feedback and risk taking. | individual and team goals accomplishments, improved team member relations and individual and team performance. |
| One-on-one coaching for team leaders (usually from someone outside of the team) | provide feedback, information and leadership training to the team leader in order to help him or her more effectively lead the team. | leadership that enables the team to focus on goal accomplishment, to quickly make decisions and to foster individual and mutual accountability among team members. |

| Intervention: | Used to: | Resulting in: |
|---|---|---|
| One-on-one coaching for team members (from someone inside or outside of the team) | provide individual feedback and temporary support to team members. | more effective participation by individual members in the team's work. Some team members may choose to or be asked to leave the team in their and the team's best interests. |

"Thanks," said Dane as he scanned the handout. "I see that training and facilitated discussion are listed here. I thought that's what trainers did."

"Many performance consultants do specialize in designing and developing training," Vance replied. "But training is the right solution only when there are gaps in skills and knowledge. It's not the solution for everything. The same is true with any of the interventions listed. They're only effective with the things for which they're intended. Anything else is a waste of people's time and money. I happen to be a performance consultant who specializes in working with teams.

"So Dane," Vance continued, "why do you think you might be in need of a performance consultant?"

Dane explained what the team was experiencing and expressed his deep concerns about its ability to meet senior management's performance expectations. He was well aware of the pressure to meet the deadlines, and he was frustrated that some team members weren't taking it more seriously. And with the new team member, Joseph, coming on board next week, more valuable time would be lost bringing him up to speed. Yet Dane was an optimist, sure the team was capable of developing innovative ideas that would improve service delivery and that they could directly connect this to improved profitability. They had already drafted some initial plans that he felt were cutting edge.

"May I make a suggestion?" Vance offered.

"Please do," Dane replied.

"First," Vance stated, "my philosophy in working with teams is this: 'Do not for the team what the team can do for itself.' Go back to the team and tell them about our discussion. Tell them that as a team member, you are concerned about the team's ability to meet the performance challenge before them. And as a way of getting back on track, ask if they would be willing to confidentially share with me their perceptions of the team's performance and their thoughts on what they believe would be helpful. If—and only if—all of them agree, then will I begin the first step of the performance consulting process. Once I have their feedback, I will summarize it and meet with the entire team to share the results and help them identify next steps."

"Agreed," Dane said. "We have a team meeting tomorrow morning, and I'll have an answer for you by tomorrow afternoon."

"By the way," Vance added as he got up to leave, "may I offer you something else—for free?"

"Sure," said Dane.

"I mentioned to you that I am a performance consultant who specializes in working with teams. Here is a list of ten questions and answers I suggest a client use when interviewing a potential performance consultant to work with their team. Just so you know, I can provide you specific answers to any of these questions." Vance grinned as he handed Dane the document. "I look forward to hearing from you tomorrow," Vance added as he left Dane's office.

## Ten Questions and Answers For Finding A Team Performance Consultant (PC)

| Ask: | Listen for: |
|---|---|
| 1. Describe your experience working with teams to boost their performance. | examples of either the PC's leadership or involvement in the consulting process as well as his or her role in delivering interventions focused on improving team results. |
| 2. Describe your process for identifying team performance issues and recommending solutions. | mention of each of the steps of the consulting process. Pay particular attention to methods to analyze and identify performance gaps. Be cautious of responses that quickly jump to conclusions or interventions. |
| 3. If you were to work with us, what information would you want to have access to? | requests for documents that describe the team's purpose, goals and work approach; feedback from the team sponsor, leader and members; factors outside of the team's control. |
| 4. How do you typically report the results of your analysis findings and recommendations? | descriptions of written summaries of findings and a collaborative discussion with the team sponsor, leader and members to interpret the findings into solutions. The PC should bring some recommendations for solutions to this discussion. |
| 5. Once interventions are selected, which ones would you personally create and deliver and for which ones might you use other resources? | key strengths the PC brings to certain interventions and other expertise he or she would draw on, such as coaching or training design and facilitation, to ensure that quality interventions are delivered. |

| Ask: | Listen for: |
|---|---|
| 6. What are some examples of team problems you've dealt with and interventions you've used to address them? | specific examples of problems, interventions, why those interventions were chosen and performance results from applying the interventions. The PC should also describe his or her role in delivering these. |
| 7. How did you and the team evaluate the effectiveness of these interventions? What were the results? | examples of how the PC gathered evaluation feedback and how the feedback was linked to the interventions. Evaluation could include reactions to the interventions applied, results individuals achieved from applying the interventions and cost-effectiveness of the interventions. |
| 8. What's been one of the most challenging team issues you've addressed? How did you handle it? | a description of a problem, analysis, intervention and results. Examples might include dealing with team problem symptoms and causes and issues outside of the team's control. |
| 9. Share an example of a team you worked with that wasn't successful and describe what happened. | a description of the problem, analysis, solution and results. Focus on what the PC learned from this situation and what he or she would do differently. |
| 10. What types of resistance have you encountered when working with teams? Who was the resistance from and how did you address it? | techniques the PC used to identify the resistance and steps taken to mitigate or resolve it. (Note: Resistance is normal and to be expected when dealing with teams.) |

At the meeting the next morning, the team had an animated discussion about what Dane shared with them. Some members felt it was unnecessary and a waste of valuable time to answer "some consultant's" questions. They didn't like the idea of being examined under a microscope, and the idea of a group hug left them feeling nauseated. Yet other team members agreed with Dane's concerns and felt that doing something was better than doing nothing. If the team was to succeed, it needed to get back on track fast. No one wanted this to be a failure. After lots of conversation, it was unanimously decided that Vance could do an electronic survey of the team members and present the feedback within ten days. At 4:00 that afternoon, Dane called Vance with the news. Two weeks later, the team was assembled to hear Vance's presentation of his findings.

After introductions, Vance began by thanking the team members for their candid feedback. He said that was a sign of their commitment to the team and to each other and that such a level of commitment would be necessary for them to succeed. Vance shared that most performance problems in teams fall within six general categories:

1. **Unclear goals**: Confusion about performance goals and targets invariably slows the team down. While goals may start out clearly defined, priorities can change as work progresses. Targets also need to change or confusion results. When that happens, teams need to revisit their team disciplines and clarify to ensure that all members have a common understanding and commitment to them.

2. **Mistaken attitudes**: In a Shared-Leadership Team, only the team succeeds and only the team fails. This is different from the attitude of "I only have to be accountable for the work that I do." Without an attitude of commitment, collective work products and shifting leadership, the team will limit its success.

3. **Missing skills**: The primary advantage of a team is its ability to bring the multiple skills and talents of all its members to produce results beyond what is possible through individual effort alone. If the right skill sets are not present among the members, the team cannot accomplish its goals.

4. **Membership changes**: Whenever a new team member is added, the other members need to integrate him or her into

the team. In a way, a new team is being formed that incorporates the ideas and perspectives of the new member. The team must develop a new shared understanding of purpose and goals.

5. **Time pressures:** Time is often a thorn in the side of a group that seeks team performance. Teams and teamwork take time as members gain a common understanding of the team disciplines. Yet from this initial investment of time come creative approaches and efficiency.

6. **Lack of discipline and commitment**: Exceptional team performance comes more from discipline and commitment than anything else. The role of self-discipline is most important. Each member must be willing to give and receive constructive feedback and coaching. If this fails, team members may need to be replaced.

After responding to team members' questions, Vance went on to share his feedback summary from the online assessment. Essentially, there were four key issues: 1) members had varying interpretations of two of the team goals and their outcomes; 2) with Kris's departure and Joseph's entrance, momentum had been lost, and there was confusion about roles; 3) procedures were not being documented, which resulted in inconsistency and the information being limited to only a couple of people; 4) everyone mentioned their concerns about the looming December 19th deadline and the team's ability to deliver.

While much of the news came as no surprise, the team members were impressed by how Vance had captured the issues in such a short time. As the team discussed how to respond to these issues, they finally agreed to set aside a day for an offsite to address them head on. They had to or they knew they would fail, and failure wasn't an option they wanted. The team agreed to meet in one week to work things through. Vance agreed to assist two members in creating the offsite agenda, although he would not attend. The team would do this together.

In retrospect, team members would remember the offsite as nothing less than a watershed moment. The discussions were refreshingly candid yet constructive. Joseph's enthusiasm was infectious, and he was immediately able to recognize some efficient ways of doing things that other team members had overlooked. Mary Ann was grateful to be looking at the faces of the other team members as they talked instead of connecting via speakerphone. Neoma suggested a way to document procedures that would save the team more time than it took. Perhaps the most poignant moment was when Rex shared that his reason for being late with his assignments was because of the extra care he was giving to his father who was suffering from Alzheimer's.

Yes, the team was back on track. The next four weeks flew by. The team not only made up the time they had lost but there was also a new sense of enthusiasm and energy among the team members that made the problems and setbacks they encountered seem minor. On the day before Thanksgiving, they were actually looking forward to their presentation to the Senior Management Group. They would meet the first thing on Monday to review the final plans and details.

When the team members assembled the following Monday and found Marie in the conference room, they knew something was wrong. Despite her strong, professional demeanor, Marie was ashen. As she began to speak, her voice trembled: "I am so sorry to tell you that Dane Franklin was killed last evening in a one-car accident. On his way home from visiting his parents, his car hit a patch of ice and went off an embankment. He died on impact." The entire room stood silent, as if enveloped by the same icy patch.

It wasn't until after they had attended Dane's funeral that the team members came together and made their decision. They knew they had to move forward with the Senior Management Group presentation—not just for Dane but for themselves. It was as simple as that. They went back to work that afternoon and resolved to do whatever it took to blow the socks off the Senior Management Group. Because they had held fast to the shared-leadership disciplines, they had everything they needed to proceed.

Every team member was in the room for the presentation. When they were finished, the team members fielded grilling questions for another thirty minutes. They answered every one and backed up their responses with detailed research. Yes, what they were proposing was bold. But wasn't that what they were asked to do? After all, their charge—service excellence— demanded innovative solutions to keep Midwestern Bank and Commerce ahead of the competition. CEO Darrell Bergstrom was the first to say it: "You have done what we have asked and more. You have created something beyond what we thought was feasible and have backed up your recommendations with solid research. With some minor exceptions and a lot of hard work ahead of us, I believe we are on the verge of a new phase of our business. Well done."

A few weeks later, the team held its final meeting, a luncheon, to celebrate and say good-bye as a team. Mary Ann flew in from Kansas City. Marie and Vance King were there. And there was one empty chair.

Mary Ann, Rex and Kathy were joining the implementation team being formed to operationalize the Service Excellence Team's strategy. Joseph had been promoted to a credit manager, and Neoma was to head up a new project in finance. Marchelle, too, was taking on a new role—mom. Her baby was due in mid-June.

As the luncheon came to a close, the team members presented Marie with a plaque. When she finished reading it, she said, "Thank you. You have learned well. Please share these lessons with others. Our organization needs you."

# Thank You For the Gift of Shared Leadership

## The Service Excellence Team

What we have learned about teams:

1. Effective teams are the most powerful resource available to boost group performance.
2. There are specific differences between Effective Work Groups, Single-Leader Teams and Shared-Leadership Teams.
3. Wise leaders are able to leverage the strengths of each team and group type based on the work to be done.
4. When performance demands the combined contributions, skills and talents of multiple people, the shared-leadership approach is most effective.
5. Team purpose and team goals are the most powerful motivators for team performance.
6. In a Shared-Leadership Team, only the team can succeed and only the team can fail.
7. Team problems are normal and to be expected. When they occur, it's up to the team to get back on track.
8. Symptoms of team performance problems are usually consequences of deeper performance issues.
9. A skilled performance consultant can assist teams in boosting their performance.
10. Do not for the team what the team can do for itself.

*In memory of Dane Franklin.*

## Lee S. Johnsen

Lee Johnsen is President of Partners In Development, a company that leverages human resources and organizational development expertise to help organizations assess employee performance and design and deliver programs that impact the bottom line. Lee has held officer and management positions in Fortune 500 corporations as well as government agencies for over 20 years. In these roles, he enhanced shareholder value by setting strategic objectives and leveraging resources to deliver excellent customer service and business results. His strong facilitation skills have assisted executives and other leaders in creating strategic business and department plans that enabled them to achieve financial and production results and improve work relationships. Lee specializes in leadership and management development, performance improvement, teambuilding, sales development, and coaching. He has developed and conducted extensive organizational and performance assessments for government and financial services organizations. Lee holds a BS degree from South Dakota State University and an MA degree in counseling from Northeast Missouri State University. He is a certified professional in Performance Technology, Human Resources, and Organizational Development. He has presented at national and international conferences and as a graduate school instructor. He currently serves on the Board of Directors for the Chicago Chapter of the American Society for Training and Development (CCASTD). Born and raised in South Dakota, Lee currently resides in Chicago.

Lee S. Johnsen
Partners In Development
4958 W. Ainslie St.
Chicago, IL 60630
Tel: 773-282-8985
Email: johnsenL@ameritech.net

# Chapter Nine

## The Wheel of Teambuilding Fortune!

### Karen Phelps

In the corporate world, where helping a teammate reach your level could potentially put you out of a job, where is the incentive to work compatibly together? Could the corporate world learn from leaders who have mastered the art of team-building in direct sales and network marketing? I think so! These leaders know the value and importance of building a strong team. Some of them have built teams of hundreds or thousands of people. Each player is responsible not only for his or her own activities but also for helping to teach and mentor new members of the team. Successful direct-sales teams have leaders who promote leaders who promote leaders and so on.

I spent more than twenty years in direct sales, and I built an incredible team. Over the years, our region held several number one positions. However, each time I was recognized as the number one leader, I held a big celebration party for my team to thank them for all their help. The simple truth is that you cannot be a top leader with your company without having an incredible team. Early in my career, I learned that the Zig Ziglar saying, "You can get everything in life you want when you help enough other people get what they want," really is true!

This chapter recognizes the techniques that successful direct-sales and network-marketing leaders around the world have been using to build and maintain powerful organizations. For years, I studied and learned what successful leaders did and applied this knowledge while building my team. Here are some of the simple yet effective ways I used to produce a dynamite team. Corporate as well as direct-sales and network-marketing leaders can apply these techniques.

## THE WHEEL OF TEAMBUILDING FORTUNE

Let's imagine that your team is a wheel with eight spokes. Each spoke is responsible for part of the weight of the wheel as it rotates. When a few of the spokes are missing, an uneven wear pattern will develop in the wheel. But if all of the spokes are in place when the wheel is revolving, the ride is pretty smooth. Now imagine that your team is the wheel, and each spoke represents a technique or principal to improve cooperation within your organization. Your team can survive if only three or four of the principles are implemented, but the ride will become bumpy over time. With each new technique that is implemented, the ride becomes smoother and smoother. The team members become content with themselves as well as the other members of the team. Life is good! So here are some of the spokes you can add to your "team wheel."

## The First Spoke—Goal Setting

The first practice I implemented early in my career was goal setting. One of my responsibilities was to help each individual who came into my organization set personal and business goals for him or herself. It's a proven fact that when people set targets for themselves they will work harder to reach them. Over fifty percent of the people who joined had never really learned how to set goals for themselves. Let's face it: Goal setting still isn't taught in most schools today, so if your parents didn't teach you about setting goals, you probably didn't learn much. I educated each individual on how to set goals and stressed the importance of having them. I soon discovered that most people really wanted to accomplish more than the minimums the job required; they just weren't sure where to begin.

What can you do? You can take time with each team member and ask where he or she would like to be in the next year or two. Do they still want to be doing the same jobs or would they like to be at the next level? Find out what you as the leader can do to help. After you have helped the new member identify a few personal and business goals you need to help him or her devise a plan of action. You will need to teach how to write a step-by-step plan to reach the target. You will also need to follow up after the initial goal-setting session. Make an appointment at least once a month to have a conversation, either in person or on the telephone, to discuss the results at that point.

Goal setting has to be constant yet always changing. Once a goal has been reached, it is important for the team member to identify a new goal so that the individual's performance is constantly improving. I found that whenever an individual in my organization reached her goal, I needed to be ready to work with her right away to set another one. A good team leader looks to the future. He or she knows that to sustain continued success for each individual as well as the team, there is a need for constant and infinite improvement.

Building a number one team was the result of working with each person individually. As I worked with each person to help her achieve the goals she had set for herself, my team continued to reach and exceed the goals that had been set for us by the company. The combined totals of each person's individual goal soon became much greater than the total goal I had set for the team. So as the members of our team began to reach and exceed their goals, our team was propelled forward.

## The Second Spoke—Training and Education

The next technique I used was to develop a duplicable system of training and educating new members. Leaders of successful direct-sales teams have mastered this technique. Ask yourself these questions:

- "How long will it take me to train this new team member?"

- "Is it easier and more productive for me to train this person individually, or is it possible to educate this new member with the rest of the new people on the team?"

- "Would it be more productive for me to do the work and have the new people observe a few times or spend my time working with each person as he or she learns the job?"

The secret is developing an easy duplicable system that can first be learned by observation and then improved upon by implementation. Are there others on the team who are doing the same job? Can they also help in the training of the new person? If so, are you letting them help in the training and education of new members? Even though some jobs are harder than others to learn, most of the time they can be learned first by observation and then by implementation. Make sure to review the performance of the new person closely within the first few weeks so that any oversight can be corrected as soon as possible. In summary, the three basic steps I used to train my team were, observation, implementation and follow-up assessment.

## The Third Spoke—Mentoring

The third element of developing your dream team is to make sure every new person on your team has a mentor. The definition of mentor is "a trusted advisor." Unfortunately, this was not a method that I implemented in the early stages of my career. In the beginning, I did more coaching than mentoring. A coach is someone who teaches or trains. Anyone can be a coach, but it takes someone special to be a mentor. Yes, we do need to teach and train and show people how to do their jobs. However, the mentoring comes into play when we listen as the other person speaks and we encourage that individual to find solutions to any challenge that arises. Becoming a mentor was one of the hardest things I ever learned to do. I, like a lot of other people, would rather talk than listen. Being a mentor means you listen to someone without judging. Being a mentor means the student can come to you with challenges or problems and you will help him or her sort through them. But you don't necessarily give them the answers. Mentors are cheerleaders! According to John Maxwell, "People don't care how much you know until they know how much you care." Each achievement, advancement or promotion brings a new reason to celebrate. One of the most satisfying and rewarding components of my direct-sales career was being able to help others on my team advance to a higher level. Mentoring is beneficial for both the mentor and the person being mentored. Both individuals will benefit from the practice and grow from the lessons that are learned.

## The Fourth Spoke—Success Tools

The fourth method used by all successful direct-sales team leaders is to provide the tools necessary for success. We already discussed goal setting and mentoring, but when you are not there, how do you provide the support and help needed? Dynamic team leaders continually seek ways to improve themselves as well ways to help members of their team. As a team leader, I had a lending library of motivational, leadership, inspirational, personal and career-development books and audiocassettes that my team could borrow. I had already made the investment when I purchased the books and tapes, so rather than have them sitting on the shelf after I was done reading or listening, I loaned my materials out to my team. I discovered that it often only took my lending someone a few items before she realized the importance of having some of these items for herself. Other people soon began to bring the materials they had purchased to our get-togethers and began sharing with other members of the team. The self-confidence and personal skills of the individuals on our team began to grow. It was amazing to watch each individual blossom after implementing some of the ideas learned from the success programs.

I've observed several organizations that now have a recommended reading and listening list for the members of their group. Each member is encouraged to purchase the same book or audio program and then after everyone has finished reading the book or listening to the audio program, they meet to discuss what they have learned from it. What a great way to help the other members of your team develop personally as well as professionally. To stay ahead of the competition, increase the confidence of your team members by encouraging participation in self-development programs

## The Fifth Spoke—Meaty Meetings

The fifth spoke on your team wheel is for meetings. Most people hate attending meetings, because they are boring, and there is often nothing new to be learned. The monthly gathering for my group provided the five key elements that every successful meeting needs to include: motivation, education, recognition, participation and *fun*! I've observed meetings that had a lot of education, a small amount of recognition and then closed with motivation, but the team members wore glazed-over expressions on their faces for eighty percent of the meeting. Most of them probably couldn't convey to you even twenty percent of what happened at the meeting.

It is not only necessary but also easy to incorporate all five ingredients into all of your meetings. The length of the meeting is not nearly as important as the content and involvement by other members. Here are some of the methods I used to produce fun, educational meetings that people loved to attend!

## *Meeting Preparation*
- Decide on the theme
- Assign Topics
- Assign Tasks

## *The Meeting*
- Have and follow an agenda
- Begin on time
- Keep each speaker on time

First, decide the theme of the meeting, how long it will be and the topics that need to be discussed. You can then plan your agenda one of two ways. You can divide the length of the meeting by the number of topics to be discussed and have an equal amount of time for each topic, or you can decide how much time is needed for each topic and allot a specific amount of time for each one. I found this was an easier method to use, because some topics might be easy to teach in five minutes whereas another subject might need fifteen minutes to be thoroughly discussed.

Next, I assigned someone to cover each topic on the agenda. Most companies and organizations would assign leaders or department heads to teach at the meetings. While I often used the top leaders on my team for different segments, I also selected at least one brand-new person who was really excited and motivated and gave her five or ten minutes to share her success story. Utilizing a new member was one of the best techniques I ever implemented. Why? New people bring fun and excitement to the organization! When you encourage them to participate in the meeting you are including them as valuable members of the team. An added benefit is that their enthusiasm and attitude generally rub off on the rest of the team! Did you ever notice how people often brighten up around a newcomer!

For several years, my meetings were a chore I wasn't too pleased about. I planned, organized and held the entire meeting by myself every month. It was really more of a control issue than anything for me. My Type A personality was showing through, and I needed to do everything myself so that it would be done correctly. Wow—when I think back on those days, I realize that those meetings were really pretty boring. It was as if I were saying to everyone, "You need to listen to me, because I know how to do it." I can't believe how wrong I was. Why did I change? I was burning out from trying to do everything myself. I held a meeting with my top people, and I told them I had a problem. The problem was I was tired of doing the work for the meetings alone, and I felt that the meetings were not as productive as they could be. I invited all of them to be a part of the solution. By then, several of the people had been in the business for a while and were perfectly capable of teaching as well, if not better, than I was. Everyone was delighted to be included as an essential player in our meetings. By the way, I quit calling them "my meetings" and started saying "our meetings." I had learned another valuable lesson. There is no "I" in "TEAM"!

Avoid falling into the trap of being the person responsible for preparing and setting up for every meeting. There is no reason to do it all yourself when there are competent and willing players to help. Arrange a rotating list of team members who will be responsible for coming early to help set up the room for the meeting. Someone different can bring snacks and beverages each month. If there is a budget for this expense, ask the person to do the shopping and bring in the receipt for reimbursement. Allow the person in charge to be creative and bring snacks that blend in with the theme of the meeting. For example, our company once offered a free trip to Hawaii for everyone who qualified by reaching a set sales goal. At the monthly meeting where we announced the trip, we arranged for a luau theme. The room was decorated Hawaiian style, and we provided tropical punch and fruit kabobs for the beverage and snack; Hawaiian shirts and grass skirts were optional attire. I do have to admit it was one of the most fun meetings we ever had, and we educated everyone on things they could do to increase their sales and their chances of earning the trip! Involve as many people as you can in each meeting. You will notice a continual sense of accomplishment as individuals become involved in the planning and preparation of each meeting.

### Meeting Components
- Education
- Recognition
- Motivation
- Participation
- Fun

The team members who have been assigned the topics do the educational part of the meeting. There are usually two to four different topics discussed depending on the length of the meeting. Too many topics create pandemonium when trying to keep a meeting on time.

Of the meeting components, recognition is probably the most critical. I'll be discussing recognition in more depth later on, but I want to discuss here the importance of having some form of recognition at every meeting. Recognition is praise for a job well done.

An individual's performance usually rises right after receiving an award or recognition. Why? Because she felt good at the time of the recognition and she wants more of it. The sooner you recognize an individual for an accomplishment, the greater the chance of improvement by her. A pattern for success will be developed early in her career and will usually continue. It's similar to the goal setting I discussed earlier in the chapter. It is by no means our intention to do worse than we did previously. So we continue to raise our goals and our production to achieve the desired results, which are a sense of accomplishment, praise and recognition. Have you ever wondered why top producers repeat the pattern over and over again? It is because they love the praise and recognition that come with being a top producer.

Everyone loves to be recognized in front of the group. That is why it is so important to give the recognition at the meeting. One more tip on this subject: Make sure you bring the person to the front of the room for proper recognition and encourage applause by starting it yourself. Also, have a camera ready to take a picture of the recipient with his or her award, and, if possible, publish it in the monthly newsletter.

The next ingredient of a successful meeting is motivation. There are many books on the subject, so assign an individual to research a specific area of motivation such as teamwork, self-confidence, encouragement, etc. and prepare a ten-minute motivational close with a call to action. Here is an example: The employee morale has been a little low lately, and you've decided that the theme of the meeting will be "Smile and the World Smiles With You." The close of the meeting could provide information on laughter and smiling and the benefits for everyone. Smiling and laughing increase our endorphins, which, in turn, help us to feel better, so the person who smiles feels good. But what about the person who is on the receiving end of the smile? Every time I see someone smiling at me, I smile back, so I feel better, too. It becomes a chain reaction, and soon, everyone begins to smile and feel better. The call to action is when you return to your job, no matter how bad your day has been; make a conscious effort to smile at everyone you see for the next week. Hey, what's the best thing that could happen? They'll all smile back, and everyone will begin to feel better.

The most important ingredient of every meeting is *fun*! I don't care how serious your business is, if you don't add some laughter and fun, your meeting will be boring for you as well as everyone in attendance. Let's continue with the same theme, "Smile and the World Smiles With You," and develop ways to continue the theme throughout the meeting. The first thing you could do is hang smiley-face posters on the wall in the meeting room. You could also provide playful items like smiley finger puppets or smiley pencils or pens for each attendee. You could play fun and upbeat music as the attendees are arriving for the meeting. I provide clapping-hand noisemakers to use when cheering and applauding accomplishments and trainers. I've even worn a "crab hat" as a visual description of how not to act! Be prepared; at the first few meetings, everyone may look at you like you are a little bit crazy, and some of the more "prim and proper" folks won't want to get involved. Give them time; I have rarely found a person who didn't jump in after the first few meetings. Once everyone realizes you are serious about not only educating but also having fun, the team will come together with unbelievable camaraderie.

To recap, the five essential ingredients needed for every meeting are education, recognition, motivation, participation and fun. I guarantee that when you hold meetings that incorporate all these elements, your team will not only learn from the meetings but they will enjoy the process.

## The Sixth Spoke—Recognition

The sixth technique for developing a successful team is recognition. I'd like to delve into the recognition portion in detail by providing you the answers to what I did, why I did it, what the results were and how you can implement it.

So let's start at the beginning. What did I recognize individuals for, and why was it important? Just as every organization should, I recognized and rewarded my team members for activities that produced results. Most companies recognize top performers, as I mentioned previously, but recognition given early in a person's career can help establish success patterns that will continue for years.

I thought about what I wanted each individual to accomplish, and I looked at how these accomplishments could help us as a team. I knew that in direct sales, developing a pattern of consistency early on was a key ingredient for success. This was a sales business, and people often get sales jobs so they don't have to go to work but can still say they have a job. I wanted the people on my sales force to go to work immediately. I knew that people stay excited about new jobs for approximately thirty days and that they can often accomplish more than seasoned veterans solely by relying on their enthusiasm. So I recognized consistency! Everyone who held the minimum amount of presentations came to the front of the room and received his or her award.

I also wanted to recognize people who had increased their production, so we had an achiever's award for people who had a percentage increase over what they did the previous month. We also had a Beat the Best trophy that everyone competed for. This trophy went to the person who had the highest individual order for the first month of the competition. Each subsequent month, the person with the highest individual order over the previous month would get a new trophy with her name and the order amount on it. If no one beat the amount from the previous month, that person remained the best until the amount was topped. Every six months, the slate was cleared and we began again. It was a fun challenge for everyone and was a way to encourage everyone to improve.

I recognized the sales achievers in my region, but I did so a little differently from other organizations. I recognized the top ten producers in two categories—rookies and pros. People started out as rookies for their first six months in the business. This gave each person an equal opportunity to be number one in sales. This was probably one of the smartest things I ever did, because I discovered that often, the top rookie for the month would be the next person to be promoted in our organization. The competition among the pros was a lot tougher. There were people on my team, who had been with the company for years, and often, they were hard to beat, but it didn't stop people from trying. It was fun competition between people who had become friends. It was exciting for me as the leader to watch the encouragement and praise the other members gave to the people who were recognized each month.

One of the most important things I gave recognition for was team performance. My region consisted of several teams that were developed by people whom I had brought into the business. As each person developed her own organization and moved up into management, she was responsible for helping the other members on her team. I began to recognize the team results as well as individual performances for my leaders. This recognition helped to keep the focus not only on growing as individuals but growing as a team. I was proud of the leaders in my region, some of which became top leaders in the company.

Recognition does not always have to come in the form of a gift. I was a practitioner of the long lost art of sending cards. I sent congratulatory cards for everything, or I sent an encouragement card if things weren't going well. A funny thing happened: The players on my team also got into the spirit of sending cards. We provided a team roster that included addresses, phone numbers and birth dates. Each time someone was promoted to the next level, she would be inundated with congratulations cards. I want you to just imagine what it would feel like to reach one of your goals and then receive congratulatory cards from just about everyone on your team. It's pretty powerful!

I feel that of all the techniques that I had put into practice, recognition helped to provide the results I was looking for at a much faster rate. I watched new people go on to become superstars because of the self-confidence they gained from the early recognition they received in their careers. Recognition is a powerful motivator, and the team leader who learns to use it lavishly will soon realize its potential. Our organization benefited and grew from the recognition that was provided. We went on to hold several number one positions for group sales during my years in direct sales!

How can you adapt this information if you are not a part of a sales organization? It's really quite simple. Decide what actions you feel, that when recognized, would produce positive results. If there has been a problem with people showing up late, you could recognize the people who have been on time for an entire month. Award a special prize that goes along with the recognition, such as a breakfast or lunch gift certificate. If you want to improve the cooperation between the people in your organization, develop an award for the Team Player of the Month. This could be given to recognize a person who goes above and beyond to help another coworker, whether it is helping to meet a deadline or pitching in when there was a personal problem at home. I have a favorite saying I use when it comes to recognition: "What gets recognized gets repeated"! Each action that you give acknowledgment for will inspire the rest of the team to work for the same recognition.

There are lots of ways to recognize the people on your team. Be creative. If you are the owner of your organization, determine the amount of money that you will put back into recognition efforts each month. If you are a department head, it's time to sit down with your boss and discuss ways you can increase performance through recognition. Let me put it to you this way: What will it cost you if your team doesn't increase its performance? Compare that to the minuscule cost of the awards and recognition you know you should be giving and decide whether it is worth it for you not to implement a recognition program within your organization. Don't forget to use greeting cards as a way of thanking and congratulating members of your team. If it's growth you are looking for, recognition could be one of the answers. It's a win-win situation for everyone!

### The Seventh Spoke—Social Activities

The seventh technique for developing teamwork within my region was to provide social activities outside of work that my team members could bring spouses, significant others or children to. I learned this idea from the first leader I had in direct sales. She always planned spectacular social events, where everyone had fun. My motto was, "People who play together stay together." I wanted to get to know the spouses and support people of my team members, and more importantly, I wanted them to get to know me. I didn't want the spouse to view me as an ogre who was only interested in making more money but as a person who was truly interested in the success of each member of my group.

The easiest way to do this was to provide some type of party or picnic where we could all get together. I planned bus trips to baseball games, summer picnics, Halloween parties and Christmas parties. I usually tried to put together two events a year. Everyone who participated had fun and developed personal relationships with the other members of the team. The spouses also began developing friendships with each other, and to this day, more than twenty-five years later, my husband and I still get together with some of the couples we socialized and traveled with early in my career. We formed friendships that continue today, even though the company we were with is no longer in business.

This idea is a simple one that you can implement with your team right away. A Christmas party or summer picnic is easy to plan, and by having each person bring a food dish, the burden is not placed entirely on you. Better yet, let the members of your team decide what they would like to do, where they would like to go and have each person volunteer to do something or bring something for the event. Make sure they plan for food, beverages, decorations, games, prizes, etc. If you're looking for an extra guest, you can always give me a call. I love to party!

## The Eighth Spoke—Togetherness

The eighth principle of efficient teamwork is promoting togetherness. I had a motto for our Region—"Alone you are good, but together we are great!" When it comes to teamwork, synergy occurs when each individual's performance blends and meshes with the performance of the other team members. Do your team members encourage and inspire each other? Do they experience a sense of accomplishment when the team has achieved a victory, such as completing a big project on time? Are they there both physically and in spirit for the others on the team? Are they committed to the success of the team as well as their own personal success? Do they enjoy working together?

Our team's quest to become the number one group for our company came about by accident. I was reviewing the monthly sales figures for all the groups in our company, and I realized that we were achieving much better sales than we had the previous year. At our monthly meeting, I asked the group where they would like to be in the rankings at the end of the six-month period (hoping it would at least be in the top ten). They unanimously thought we should be number one! Wow! I wasn't quite sure about this. We were behind and only had about four months left to complete the task. What if we settled for being in the top five? They wouldn't hear of it; everyone wanted to be a part of a number one team. We rallied together and came up with several ideas for how to increase our sales, most of which involved members increasing their personal performances. We made a commitment to help as many new people as possible move into leadership positions, which would help us tremendously in sales also. Several of us had attended a quarterly meeting, and when our team was announced as being number one for the previous month, pandemonium broke out. We celebrated, but just like in sports playoffs, we knew we had to continue the pattern. On the drive home, several members purchased a gift for me, and everyone autographed it as members of the Number One Team. I still have that gift today, and it always brings back good memories! We were number one during that six-month period, and more people in our group were promoted than ever before. We all experienced the thrill of what it was like to come together as a team.

I loved those days! I enjoyed watching as each new member's skills and confidence grew! I reveled in the camaraderie that we had developed. I realized that being a part of the team was what it was all about!

I didn't know much about teamwork when I began my direct-sales career. As I stated in the beginning, I read and studied everything I could about teamwork. I put into practice the elements I felt would produce the best results for the individual team players as well as the entire team. The principles and techniques I have described worked for our team. Can they work for your team as well? Absolutely. All it takes is making sure you have all the spokes in place. When your team takes time to implement goal setting, duplicable training, mentoring, motivation, educational and fun meetings, recognition, social activities and togetherness, it will become a powerful force. Keep in mind the eight spokes of teamwork, and your wheel will roll effortlessly along.

## About The Author

### Karen Phelps

Karen Phelps teaches individuals, leaders and companies to reach their "peak" performance by applying tested and proven techniques that were used by her and her Direct Selling team to achieve results. For over twenty years Karen excelled in and accepted awards for both personal and team sales performance. Year after year she coached the individuals on her team as she helped them to reach the goals they had set for themselves. In doing so she also reached several of her own team goals including holding several number one titles. Karen's topics include leadership, teambuilding, life balance, self-confidence and Direct Selling skills. Karen is definitely an individual who has "walked the talk". Her highly entertaining, interactive and high-content presentations provide her audiences with basic steps that will increase their personal as well as team performance. Karen's clients include Arbonne Int., Rainbow Child Development, BodyWise Int., Michigan Chapter of Employee Involvement Association, Michigan District of Kiwanis International, Mount Elliott Cemetery Association, Michigan Real Estate Investors Conference and Oriflame, where she spoke to the top 500 leaders worldwide at their Diamond Conference.

Karen Phelps
Phelps Positive Performance Inc.
4041 Baybrook
Waterford, MI 48329
Telephone & Fax: 248-673-3465
Email: Karen@Karenphelps.com
www.Karenphelps.com